10-23-21

You are
" FREE   INDEED "

Dis Cont & Linda

Cover Concept
Tabatha J. Enterprises
admin@tabathaj.com

Typing and Editing
Charlotte Harris

Layout and Finishing
Gwendolyn Brown
EHP Creations, Nashville, TN

Published by:
Alpha & Omega Innovative Publishing
www.aoinnovativepublishing.com

Printed in the United States of America
July 2021

Although the author and publisher have made every effort to ensure that the information in this book was correct at press time, the author and publisher does not assume and hereby disclaim any liability to any party for any loss, damage, or destruction caused by errors or omissions, whether such errors or omissions result from negligence, accident, or any cause.

All rights reserved. No part of this book may be reproduced or utilized in any form or by any means, electronic or mechanical, including photocopying and recording or by any information storage and retrieval system without permission in writing from the publisher.

TABLE OF CONTENTS

INTRODUCTION 9

CHAPTER 1
DARK SHADOWS 13

CHAPTER 2
FORGETTING 25

CHAPTER 3
LOOKING FORWARD 33

CHAPTER 4
PRESS ON 39

CHAPTER 5
WHAT IS YOUR PAIN LEVEL FROM 1-10? 45

CHAPTER 6
I HAVE ISSUES 57

CHAPTER 7
CTRL + ALT + DEL (Control+ Alt + Delete) 71

CHAPTER 8
LETTING GO 81

CHAPTER 9
FANNING THE FLAMES 89

CHAPTER 10
YOU'RE GOING TO MAKE IT AFTER ALL 101

CONCLUSION..109

INTRODUCTION

TWO LITTLE SHADOWS

I saw a young mother
With eyes full of laughter
And two little shadows came following after.
Wherever she moved,
They were always right there
Holding onto her skirts,
Hanging onto her chair.
Before her, behind her -
An adhesive pair.

"Don't you ever get weary
As, day after day,
Your two little tagalongs
Get in your way?"

She smiled as she shook
Her pretty young head,
And I'll always remember
The words that she said.

SHADOWS OF THE PAST

> "It's good to have shadows
> That run when you run,
> That laugh when you're happy
> And hum when you hum-
> For you only have shadows
> When your life's filled with sun."
>
> *Author Unknown - Public Domain*

Shadows are dark and can be scary, but you cannot have a shadow without sunlight. A shadow is a dark area where light from a light source is blocked by an opaque object. It occupies all of the three-dimensional volume behind an object with light in front of it. The cross-section of a shadow is a two-dimensional silhouette of a reverse projection of the object blocking the light. That dark area is called a shadow.

Every living human being has a shadow. Even an object or an animal has a shadow. Have you ever watched a toddler as he discovers his shadow for the first time? There is something so pure and innocent about the whole encounter. They either try to run from it or proceed to chase it. The toddler is genuinely surprised that the shadow is following him! Discovering the shadow is a fascinating event for most children. There is such a thrill and wonder in watching it change shape and direction. The fear of their shadow often passes quickly, and they begin to enjoy hand-shadow games.

In our book, **"Shadows of The Past,"** we want to shed

INTRODUCTION

light on the dark hidden traumatic events that lurk and linger around us. We find that these traumatic events have become as much a part of us as our own shadow. We try to run from them but to no avail. They follow us everywhere we go. In this book we want to show you how to become victorious over every shadow of your past. There is hope. Jesus died and rose from the grave with power over our past mistakes, present mistakes and future mistakes. Because He overcame, you will also overcome these shadows of the past.

Regrets and mistakes can become shadows that burden your life and paralyze your future. We've all had our share of them. In fact, they are a part of life. Ask anyone about their regrets and you will find they all can think of one thing they wish they had done differently. You cannot undo or redo what has been done. The shadows of your past do not have to control your future. Remember, they are only shadows. There is no life in that shadow. It's a reminder, not a reality. It's a silhouette not the real masterpiece.

Shadows are powerless reflections of the mistakes and regrets of your past. As long as they are around, we are reminded of the mistakes and choices we made. We are also reminded of the trauma they brought to our lives. Our minds are programmed to keep fragments of the past alive, therefore creating a shadow that is a constant reminder. We keep replaying scenes and rewriting our narrative. With repetition, we give energy to these shadows. It is time for these shadows to fade into obscurity. The past is gone. It has no life. So stop identifying with that shadow. It is not who you are now.

SHADOWS OF THE PAST

It is time for the shadows to stop following you around. Deliverance is real and deliverance is NOW! Healing is NOW! Freedom is NOW! *"Now unto Him that is able to keep you from falling, and to present you faultless before the presence of his glory with exceeding joy."* **(Jude 24-25 KJV)** God is able, and he will release you from the shadows of the past. No longer will they stalk you and remind you of past failures.

The struggle is over! It's time to move on!

Shadows of the past tend to remind you of your "younger you." The immature, "foolish" and not so smart you. If that is a description of who you were, don't allow that "younger you" shadow to yet control your life. Our "younger selves" have taught us some lessons and have gotten us to where we are today.

In this book we want you to get the revelation of the power of forgiveness. Evidently Jesus thought you were worthy of forgiveness. If he thought otherwise, he would not have laid down his life for you. Don't allow shadows to haunt you. The sun will shine again! You can't have a shadow without the sun, and you can't have true healing from the past without **THE SON! (JESUS)**

1 DARK SHADOWS

There was a popular television soap opera series called **Dark Shadows.** It was a daytime television series that ran from 1966 to 1971 on ABC. It spanned 1,225 episodes and saw several off-shoots including a series of novels, comics, and audio dramas. Dark Shadows was also re-made for television in 1991.

With its alluring tales of Gothic mystery and supernatural intrigue, Dark Shadows became the most popular daytime series of all time during its run. The show's most popular character was Barnabus Collins, a vampire. Dark Shadows became a pop-culture phenomenon, introducing the world to the introspective vampire. The show was centered around vampires, werewolves, witches and warlocks. It was a very "dark" television series that piqued the interest of millions of people. There were always strange events and mysteries occurring at the Collins' estate mention.

Much like this popular television soap opera, Dark Shadows, we all have experienced dark shadows of the past that tend to have a life of its own. The television series, "Dark Shadows" was centered around the past and the loss of love. It was about how things became as they were.

Many people struggle with dark shadows of bitterness, anger, unforgiveness, rejection, guilt, abuse, etc. Just like it's hard to kill a vampire (in folklore, mystical tales), so it is hard to get rid of dark shadows of the past. Many of them remain for years. Let's look at how these dark shadows of the past affect our lives.

BITTERNESS

Bitterness is usually associated with anger and grudges, and it is poisonous. Bitterness is often a result of some past event which has hurt, scarred and jaded the person. Research gives credence to the link between state of mind and health. Bitterness can make a person ill. Holding onto bitterness can affect metabolism, immune response or organ function and lead to physical disease, according to researchers. There's a saying "absence makes the heart grow fonder," but bitterness makes the heart grow sicker. The latter statement has validity and is true. Studies have proven this. Your state of mind may have a significant impact on your health and well-being. Bitterness is a dark shadow that can be relentless.

Psychologists have for some time observed that feelings like anger, hostility, envy, bitterness and hate evoke the stress response. If these feelings are persistent, the body's capability to stay healthy and fight off illness can become impaired. We can improve our own well-being by letting go of hostility and bitterness.

The Bible deals with every emotion, every behavior, and every circumstance we may face in life, including bitterness.

"See to it that no one falls short of the grace of God and that no bitter root grows up to cause trouble and defile many. (Hebrews 12:15 NIV)

Not only is bitterness a dark shadow, but it is also a root. A root is that part of a plant which attaches to the ground and support the plant. It typically is underground, conveying water and nourishment to the rest of the plant via numerous branches and fibers. This description of bitterness being a root; according to the Bible is a very serious issue. The root is the basic cause, source and origin of something. Let's slow the row on this boat. Let's get into "sloth mode" for a moment. Bitterness is a root! It attaches itself to you like a dark shadow. It supports your decision to be bitter. It provides a nourishment of anger and unforgiveness to your soul. It defiles your entire body, soul, and spirit, causing you to miss the mark of grace that has been afforded to you. Is bitterness really worth holding onto?

C.S. Lewis said, "getting over a painful experience is much like crossing monkey bars. You have to let go at some point in ordered to move forward." Bitterness starts out small, but then an offense burrows its way into our hearts. Watch out for that dark shadow of offense, because it causes us to replay the offense over and over in our minds. Then we retell the hurt in detail to anyone that will listen. Now we have support that pushes us further into the bitterness

Have you ever been offended? Could it be possible that you are a "Frequent Flyer?" (Always offending others or always getting offended). Well, Frequent Flyer, it's time for you to get delivered. Do you recall the feeling you have when you hear the offended person's name? You get an unsettling angry feeling just hearing their name mentioned. You look for any reason, real and imagined to dislike them. With every piece of new information you get, you dislike them even the more and there goes the layer of bitterness. The dark shadow is cast, and you have a new tag-along called bitterness.

When you are offended or disappointed by someone and you allow the hurt to germinate in your heart, the dark shadow of bitterness and resentment will take root. Maya Angelou says this about bitterness, "Bitterness is like cancer. It eats upon the host." Be determined not be a host to bitterness. It invites a whole host of other guests like toxic emotions, jealousy, anger, hatred, disobedience, rage and gossip. Jesus has shown us a better way, and that way is love.

> "Love is patient, love is kind. It does not envy, it does not boast, it is not proud. It does not dishonor others; it is not self-seeking. It is not easily angered; it keeps no record of wrongs." "Love does not delight in evil but rejoices with the truth. It always protects, always trusts, always hopes, always perseveres."
>
> "Love never fails. But where there are prophecies, they will cease; where there are tongues, they will be stilled, where there is knowledge, it will pass away."
>
> "And now these three remain, faith, hope, and love. But the greatest of these is love." (1Corinthians 13:4-13 NIV)

We always have a choice. We can get rid of the dark shadow of bitterness, and we can become better. Allow God to pluck up that root of bitterness and replace it with love. The Psalmist writes, *"Create in me a clean heart, O God, and renew a right spirit within me." (Psalm 51:10)*

Walking in love and forgiveness can eliminate the shadow of bitterness. Recovery from deeply rooted or intense bitterness may be as complex as the reason for the bitterness, but Jesus has provided a way out from under that dark shadow. In *James 4: 7 (KJV)* we are told,

> *"Submit yourselves therefore to God. Resist the devil, and he will flee from you. "Draw nigh to God, and he will draw nigh to you. "Humble yourselves in the sight of the Lord and he shall lift you up".*

Here are your four keys to freedom:
- Submit (to God)
- Resist (the devil)
- Draw nigh (to God)
- Humble (yourself).

UNFORGIVENESS

This is a dark shadow of your past that creates an emotional storm in your life. Feelings such as stress, anxiety, depression, insecurity, and fear will all surface and derail your success. Unforgiveness also creates a hardened heart towards the offender. The best definition for unforgiveness is the unwillingness to forgive someone for hurting, betraying, breaking your trust, or causing you intense emotional pain.

Ask yourself this question. Can I afford not to forgive? Here are some compelling reasons why you should forgive. People that carry unforgiveness in their heart are very susceptible to physical and emotional problems such as high blood pressure, cancer, arthritis, decreased immune response, anxiety and depression, as well as other mental illnesses. Unforgiveness is such a dark lonely shadow that inprisons you, isolating you from living your best life.

Unforgiveness is like a toxic margarita drink mixture of anger, resentment, bitterness, hatred, self-judgment and self-sabotage, all mixed and shaken together. Dr. Martin Luther King Jr. said, "Forgiveness is not an occasional act, it is a constant attitude." This shadow loves to follow the offended hurt person. In pretense that everything is okay. You think you're over it. You know something isn't quite right, and you can't stop thinking about what happened. You can't seem to move on. Admit it, you have not forgiven that person that hurt you and part of you want them to feel the same pain they have caused you.

There is a story in the Bible that teaches us a lesson on how many times we should forgive those who offend us. It is the parable of the unmerciful servant. It is found in **Matthew Chapter 18:21-35.**

> *"Then Peter came to Jesus and asked, "Lord how many times shall I forgive my brother or sister who sins against me? Up to seven times?" "Jesus answered, I tell you not seven times, but seventy- seven times. Therefore, the kingdom of heaven is like a king who*

wanted to settle accounts with his servants. As he began the settlement a man who owed him 10,000 bags of gold was brought to him. Since he was not able to pay, the master order that he and his wife and his children and all that he had be sold to repay the debt.

At this time the servant fell on his knees before him. Be patient with me, he begged, and I will pay back everything. The servant's master took pity on him, canceled the debt and let him go. But when the servant went out he found one of his fellow servants who owed him 100 silver coins. He grabbed him and began to choke him, "Pay back what you owe me." He demanded. His fellow servant fell to his knees and begged him, "Be patient with me and I will pay it back. But he refused. Instead he went off and had the man thrown into prison until he could pay his debt. When the other servants saw what had happened, they were outraged and went and told their master everything that had happened. Then the master called the servant in. "You wicked servant he said, I canceled all that debt of yours because you begged me too. Shouldn't you have had mercy on your fellow servant just as I had on you? In anger his master handed him over to the jailers to be tortured until he should pay back all he owed. "This is how my Heavenly Father will treat each of you unless you forgive your brother or sister from your heart."

Don't let this dark shadow destroy your destiny. Forgiveness is a decision we make every day. Yes, it's hard. It's not easy getting rid of that shadow that lives with you every day. Every now and then, when you are feeling confident and strong, that shadow of unforgiveness pops out and remind you of how defeated you are. Many people spend years and even decades hanging onto offenses. Decide today not to spend another minute on unforgiveness.

We must learn to forgive from the heart. God expects us to forgive others just as he has forgiven us. There is no loophole or wiggle room to get out of this. We are commanded to love, and we are commanded to forgive. God loves our offender just as much as he loves us. He died for us all. Jesus came to save sinners. We all have sinned and fell short. Most of the New Testament in the Bible was written by a man who killed Christians. The apostle Paul killed Christians. The book of Acts (7:58) reports him as holding the coats of those who were stoning the deacon, Stephen. That's right, the apostle Paul was there. He was feared and hated by many, but God loved him and had a plan for his life. So today decide to cut loose that shadow of unforgiveness and live in the newness of life.

REJECTION

This shadow comes in many forms. Nevertheless, it is still a haunting shadow that can follow you and attach itself to you for the rest of your life. Whether the rejection you experience is large or small, one thing is for certain, it always hurts, and it usually hurts more than we expect it to.

Psychologist have found rejection to be the most common wound we sustain in life. Our risk of rejection used to be limited to the size of our social circle. Today however, that has changed due to the social media platforms and electronic communications and dating apps. Here we are connected to thousands of people who might affect us in a negative way by ignoring our texts, posts, chats, dating profiles, photos, etc. This would be considered "minor" rejections. Although to some people it may be a major rejection. Clearly there are more serious devastating rejections that can occur such as when our spouse leaves or cheat on us or divorce us. When a boyfriend or girlfriend ends the relationship. When we get fired from our jobs. When we get ostracized by our families and friends. The pain we feel is absolutely devastating and paralyzing.

This shadow of rejection is so dark, and it can cripple you for life. Whether the rejection is small or great, it does affect you in some way. Why are we so bothered by our social media friend not "liking" our post or pictures? Why in the world would we feel some kind away about that? Why would it ruin our mood for the day? It's something that is insignificant, or it should be insignificant.

Scientist have made a discovery. Our brains are wired to respond to rejection. When scientist place people in an MRI machine and ask them to recall a recent rejection, they discovered the same areas of our brain become activated when we experience physical pain. That is amazing! That is why even small rejections hurt more than we think they should because they elicit literal pain although it's emotional.

Emotional pain is only one of the ways rejection impacts our well-being. The shadow of rejection also damages our mood and self-esteem. It elicits anger and aggression as well. Unfortunately, the greatest damage the shadow causes is usually self-inflicted. Our natural response to being dumped by a mate or not making a team causes us to become self-critical. We tend to look more critically at our shortcomings and failures. Doing this is emotionally unhealthy and psychologically self-destructive.

Honestly, we've all done this at one time or another. There is good news for you! You don't have to deal with that shadow of rejection following you for the rest of your life. When your self-esteem has been hit hard, remind yourself of what God's word says. Build yourself up on a consistent daily routine of the word of God. *"Know that the Lord, he is God! It is he who made us, and we are his, we are his people, and the sheep of his pastures.* **(Psalm 100:3 ESV)**

We must remind ourselves every day, "who" we are and "whose" we are. We belong to God. We are his children. When the shadow of rejection comes, remind yourself that you are more than a conqueror.

> *"What then shall we say in response to these things? If God is for us, who can be against us? He who did not spare his own Son, but gave him up for us all- how will he not also, along with him, graciously give us all things?" "Who will bring any charge against those whom God has chosen? It is God who justifies. Who then is the one who condemns? No one. Christ Jesus who died- more than that, who was raised to life is at the right hand of God and is also*

interceding for us." Who shall separate us from the love of Christ? Shall trouble or hardship or persecution or famine or nakedness or danger or sword?

As it is written: "For your sake we face death all day long; we are considered as sheep to be slaughtered. No, in all these things we are more than conquerors through him who loved us. For I am convinced that neither death nor life, neither angels nor demons, neither the present nor the future, nor any powers, neither height nor depth, nor anything else in all creation will be able to separate us from the love of God that is in Christ Jesus our Lord." **(Romans 8:31-39)**

Nothing can separate you from God's love. Rejection can't, bitterness can't, and dark shadows certainly can't!

There it is in a nutshell! You are loved! You are blessed! You are accepted! You are more than a conqueror!

SHADOWS OF THE PAST

2 FORGETTING . . .

Forgetting the past and looking forward to what lies ahead . . . (Philippians 3:13)

I think we've all heard the saying; I will forgive, but I can't forget. What does that actually mean? Is it even possible to truly forgive someone of the hurt they caused you but not forget? It's helpful to understand the difference between forgiving and forgetting. To forgive signifies you understand that just as God has forgiven you, he expects you to forgive others. It's the principle of reciprocity. We are commanded to forgive. **Ephesians 4:32** says *"Be kind and compassionate to one another, forgiving each other, just as in Christ God forgave you."* **Matthew 6:14** says *"For if you forgive other people when they sin against you, your heavenly Father will also forgive you."*

And how can we forget "The Lord's Prayer," **Matthew 6:12,** *"and forgive us our trespasses as we forgive them that trespass (sin) against us."*

Forgiveness means you understand that all humans are imperfect and make mistakes. To "forget" is an entirely different story. Honestly, the offense is never fully forgotten. You are a spiritual being living in a natural body. You've been given a brain with the capacity of retaining information. This is called "memory." From the moment we are born, our brains are bombarded by an immense amount of information about ourselves and the world around us. We hold on to everything we've learned and experienced through memories.

Humans retain different types of memories for different lengths of time. Short term memories last seconds to hours while long-term memories last for years. We also have a working memory, which lets us keep something in our minds for a limited time by repeating it. For example, whenever you say a phone number to yourself over and over again to remember it, you're using your working memory.

Declarative memory also called explicit memory; consists of the sorts of memories you've experienced consciously. Hence, "forgetting" is not based on the way our brain has been wired. However, when we forgive from the heart, we don't get amnesia in the process. We remember the act of offense or betrayal, but we don't retain it to hold over someone's head. We let it go and move on. We take no prisoners in the process. We release them of the wrong they've done, and we release ourselves of the wrong we've done. By choosing not to dwell on whatever (or whoever) it is you're trying to forgive and forget, you allow yourself to move past that shadow that wants to imprison you. Holding on to anger and resentment doesn't hurt the other person, it hurts you.

When you forget, you are allowing yourself to walk away from that shadow and move on. You will no longer be held captive by the pain and anger of the past. The same goes for forgetting. You are no longer tortured by replaying the negative event that took place. Forgetting means casting down imaginations. Once again, this function takes place in the brain. Imagination involves a network that helps share information across different regions of the brain. The same parts of the brain involved in understanding the world around us are involved in creating mental pictures of that world. Meaning that what we imagine is shaped by what we see all the time. Our imagination allows us to do more than just daydream. It sparks new ideas and helps us visualize ourselves achieving that next great goal in life. Scientist have found that when you use your imagination, you're really firing up a lot of brain power!

All of this scientific research on imagination is good to know. It is also important that we understand satan is a master at the "power of suggestion." He knows how to suggest thoughts into your mind and cause you to believe the thoughts that's been planted into your mind.

Psychologists have studied this for years. Research has shown that deliberate suggestion can influence how people perform on learning and memory tasks, which products they prefer, and how they respond. It is found that suggestions can shape your reality. In other words, once you expect something to happen, your behaviors, thoughts, and reactions will actually contribute to making that expectation occur. For example, if you think you'll win a race, you are more likely to train, prepare and perform in a way that gives you a greater chance of winning. As we struggle to forgive and forget, we must be aware that satan does not want you to forgive and forget. He wants you to hold on to the offense and justify the need to remain angry.

The battlefield to forgive and forget lies in the heart and mind. You don't have to willingly replay hurtful events in your mind, the devil will gladly do it for you. You can't stop a plane from flying over your head, but you can get out of the way and prevent it from landing on top of you. We have a saying, "Give no lie, or negative thought permission to land." Every pilot gets clearance from the air traffic controllers to land. Until they get clearance, they must continue to either circle around or maintain a holding position. You can't stop the devil from circling over your mind, but you can restrict him from landing. It's simple, but it's a challenge. Tell the devil **"This is a no-fly zone!"**

> *"We use our powerful God tools for smashing warped philosophies, tearing down barriers erected against the truth of God, feeding every loose thought and emotion and impulse into the structure of life shaped by Christ."* **(2 Corinthians 10:5 MSG)**

The Bible gives us wisdom on how to be victorious in our minds. If you are victorious in your mind, you will be victorious in your life. As your thoughts go, so will your life. So just in case you are not sure what you should be thinking on, there are some specific scriptures you can use as a guide or model for positive thinking.

> *"Finally believers, whatever is true, whatever is honorable and worthy of respect, whatever is right and confirmed by God's word, whatever is pure and*

wholesome, whatever is lovely and brings peace, whatever is admirable and a good repute, if there is any excellence, if there is any worthy of praise, think continually on these things,(center your mind on them and implant them in your hearts)"
(Philippians 4:8 AMP)

You have to choose to forget the past and plan to forget the past. This is your first step in moving on to a healthy and whole lifestyle. You don't have to live with that shadow replaying your past as if it occurred yesterday. For your mental health's sake forget the past! Yes, it was traumatic! Yes, you were abused! Yes, it hurt like Hades!

But let it go! Fight for your freedom! God wants you healed, whole and free. He has given you power and authority over every dark shadow that's assigned to your destiny. You can become stronger and better through this. Your past falls under the category of all things working together for your good. **(Romans 8:28)**

The Bible did not say that all things were good, nor did it say that all things work well. What it says is, *"And we know that in all things God works for the good of those who love him, who have been called according to his purpose."* Therefore, all things are not good. War is not good. The death of a loved one is not good. The loss of a business is not good. Drug addiction is not good. Cancer is not good. The Bible says, *"We know that all things work together for good."*

God is much like a chemist. God takes things that in and of themselves are bad, and he puts them together just as a chemist might take chemicals that in and of themselves, may be harmful and mixes them to make a medicine that brings healing. Cyanide of itself is poisonous. Mold of itself is harmful but mixed with other chemicals you get penicillin. Most of us have some salt with our meals. Table salt is made up of both sodium and chloride. By itself sodium is a deadly poison, and so is chloride. Put them together, and you have table salt. Salt gives flavor to food and a certain amount of salt is necessary for health and life. We cannot live without some salt in our systems. What are we actually saying? As much as we don't like test and trials, and adversity, we need them! You might give a rebuttal to that statement and say, "I need a test and trial like I need a hole in my head!" We feel you! None of us welcome suffering, devastation and loss, but it is needed in the mixture to work. We have to take the rainstorm with the sun in order to get a rainbow.

God can take those things that are bad and work them all together for your good and give you the victory. The end result is always victory over every circumstance. The Apostle starts out by saying and we know...This is not perhaps we know or maybe we know. This is a knowing and a certainty. It is not even hope. We don't hope that all things work together for our good; we know all things work together for good!

How can we forget Joseph in the Bible? There was certainly a lot of "forgetting" he had to do. The shadows of his past probably followed him every day for years. The things this young man experienced was unimaginable. He was betrayed by his brothers, thrown in a pit and then sold as a slave. He was lied on and accused of rape, then thrown in prison. How does anyone even begin to escape these shadows?

Forgetting the injustice, the treachery, and the downright hatred and jealousy is asking a lot. **But God Always Keeps His Promises!** It doesn't matter how dark your past is God will work all things together for your good because you love him, and you are called according to his purpose. There was a purpose for all the suffering and madness Joseph experienced. **(Genesis 37-50)**

> *"Then Joseph said to his brothers, come close to me. When they had done so, he said I am your brother Joseph, the one you sold into Egypt! And now do not be distressed and do not be angry with yourselves for selling me here, because it was to save lives that God sent me ahead of you." But God sent me ahead of you to preserve a remnant on earth and to save your lives by a great deliverance. So then it was not you who sent me here, but God."* **(Genesis 45:4-8 NIV)**

In essence, Joseph was quoting Romans chapter 8. What Satan meant for evil God turned it around for everyone's good.

In the story, we see God using every bad situation and turning it around for Joseph's good. We also see the purpose of God prevailing in the end. It was not all about Joseph; it was about saving his family and every generation thereafter. It was about saving and preserving an entire nation.

You might have a lot of "forgetting" and "forgiving" to do. Perhaps you've tried and tried, and those shadows of the

SHADOWS OF THE PAST

past are still hanging onto you. Don't give up. God can, and he will make you whole. He did it for Joseph and he will do it for you. There is a purpose for the pain and suffering. There was a purpose for the abuse and rejection. Don't faint now! You're about to see the goodness of the Lord in the land of the living!

3 LOOKING FORWARD

"Forgetting the past and looking forward to what lies ahead." (Philippians 3:13 NLT)

Life can be pretty dull and boring if you have nothing to look forward to. That's exactly what "hope" is. It is a feeling of expectation and anticipation. It is a deep desire for something to happen. Notice the Apostle said, **"Forgetting the past and looking forward or reaching forward to what lies ahead."** Hope says, "these dark shadows will not control my future." I have brighter days ahead. Hope is optimism that things will get better. It is more than just a wish. In the Bible hope is a confident assurance or expectation of what God has promised will certainly come to pass. *(Hebrews 11:1)*

Hope not only makes a tough situation more bearable, it helps us envision a better future, delivered from shadows of the past. Hope is a common desire in everyone. We all hope for something. It's an inherent part of being human. Even the rich and wealthy hope for something. It's not all about money or fame and fortune. It's about a desire in our hearts to be better, feel better, have better, and live better. None of us have it all, otherwise why would we hope. Many rich and famous people fight shadows of their past too. They deal with issues and have struggles just like everyone else.

Hope helps us define what kind of future we want. It is a part of the self-narrative that we create about how we move forward. Many people associate help with spirituality, having faith and hope in God. It is associated with prayer, making it very spiritual. For those that are not spiritual, it means that one must look on the bright side expecting the best. Hope sees challenges as opportunities.

How can we really move forward without hope? How can you look forward to something you don't desire? Some call it being optimistic. Hope is not the same as optimism. There is a difference. An optimistic person is generally more hopeful than others. On the other hand, the most pessimistic person can still be hopeful about something. Hope is not just optimistic, it's specific and focused, usually on one issue.

The key to forgetting the past and looking forward to the future is to focus on where you're going. What is the one thing you are striving to achieve? What changes do you need to make to achieve that goal? Hope is a good thing but moving forward is going to cost you something. Be prepared to channel all your energy in bringing this to fruition. Hope cannot be just for a dire situation. You can "hope" to get out of a messy relationship or some other difficulty. These dire situations could be temporary issues, or long-term situations. For example, a child hopes to get a new bike for Christmas. A girl hopes she gets a call from her admirer. An actor hopes he gets the part in a Broadway play. These are all temporal things.

The American Psychological Association studied children who grew up in poverty. They followed the children in their study and found they all had success later in life because of hope. The research concluded that hope involves planning, motivation, and determination. Notice the key elements to success: planning, motivation, and determination. Forgetting the past involves planning, motivation, and determination as well. There is no moving forward without these key elements.

Everybody has a past. Some pasts are worse than others. You can rest assured there is a spot and a blemish on even the best of us. No one is perfect because life is not perfect. Life really can leave you bitter. It can leave you feeling like "roadkill."

Life can leave you broken and crushed in a thousand pieces. Let's not forget the guilt and shame that so deeply wound the soul. It takes a lot of forgetting to move past all of this. It takes courage and determination to walk out from under those shadows. Forgiving and forgetting can seem paramount and impossible. For many that have suffered loss, the pain is so deep that they can't envision life getting any better. They adjust to the pain and the loss in an attempt to just live and struggle another day. This does not have to be you! You can come out of this deep dark dismal pit. You're not stuck in the shadows of the past. You can live your best life free from the pain and disappointments of the past.

The Bible is a holy book but many in the Bible were not holy. They were flawed. Consider the 12 disciples that were chosen. These men became the pioneering leaders of the New Testament church, but they were not without faults and failures. Not one of the chosen apostles was a scholar or rabbi. They had no extraordinary skills nor were they refined. They were ordinary people just like us. Some were liars, traitors, adulterers, murderers, ungodly and unholy. They were all these things and more. The good news is that they were (past tense). They didn't remain the same. Their lives were dramatically changed when they had a "God encounter." They became disciples of Jesus Christ. God sees and knows everything about us, and he yet loves us. He's the only one who knows exactly what we are capable of.

God chose these men with all their shortcomings because he had a purpose for their lives. They would be the ones to fan the flames of the gospel that would spread all over the earth and turn the world upside down. It is because of these chosen men that the fire of the gospel spread for centuries. To this day, there is no stopping the good news of Jesus Christ. He gave his life to save man and set them free from every bondage and every shadow of the past.

> *"The scroll of the prophet Isaiah was handed to him. Unrolling it, he found the place where it was written. The Spirit of the Lord is on me, because he has anointed me to preach good news to the poor. He has sent me to proclaim liberty to the captives and recovery of sight to the blind, to release the oppressed, to proclaim the year of the Lord's favor."* **(Luke 4:17-18)**

In this prophecy, the Messiah announced that he came to

preach the gospel to the poor, to heal the brokenhearted, to proclaim liberty to the captives, recovery of sight to the blind, to set at liberty those who are oppressed and to proclaim the acceptable year of the Lord (The Year of Jubilee).

It's time to move forward and set new achievable goals for your life. It is not the end of the world. Here are some tips for moving forward:

- Refocus and reset your life. It's time to change your mindset. Your life will move in the direction of your thoughts and your words. Whatever you set your mind and focus on is what your life and emotions will follow.
- Start speaking good things about yourself and your life. Eliminate all negative vibes and energy and accentuate the positive.
- Cut off friendships that are not in line with where you're trying to go. It's not a crime to do that. Negative friends cannot move forward with you. Silence all negative voices.
- Let go of all grudges. Holding a grudge against someone is like eating poison and expecting someone else to die. Grudges keep you holding onto the past.
- Lay aside the weights and the sin that's slowing you down. Athletes don't run a race with bricks in a backpack. If you are ready to move forward, you must lay aside those weights. What is it that's holding you back? Is it shame, regrets, failure, heartbreaks or forgiveness? What burden is too heavy to carry? God wants to lighten your load. A fresh new start is awaiting you. The time of God's favor is now. Your set time is now!

> "*Arise (from spiritual depression to a new life), shine (be radiant with the glory and brilliance of the Lord), for your light has come, and the glory and brilliance of the Lord has risen upon you."* ***(Isaiah 60:1 AMP)***

4 PRESS ON

"I press on to reach the end of the race and receive the heavenly prize for which God through Christ Jesus is calling us." (Philippians 3:14 NLT)

The Apostle states *"I press toward (press on) ... the mark for the prize..."*

Forgetting the past is the first step in deliverance and healing. Leaving behind shadows of the past is a process. It's not a sprint. We do not mean to give you the impression that forgetting the past is as simple as popping your fingers. Although some people find that skill difficult. Forgetting the past is hard and it requires work. It requires determination. So be ready to persevere for the long-haul.

The Apostle Paul uses the analogy of a runner who is focused on the prize ahead of him. Paul's focus is on forward momentum, not prior mistakes. He realizes that getting hung up on the past is unfruitful and frustrating. You cannot move ahead if your thoughts are focused on the past. Paul's goal was clear and precise. Heaven, the ultimate reward, was his goal. He understood he must continue to run his race (pursuing Christ) until he meets him face-to-face.

All Olympic runners are contesting for the highest prize.

Not a single runner trains and endures strenuous exercises and workouts with the intention or goal of winning the least prize. Their goal is to win the highest prize, the gold medal. They have one goal in mind; therefore, their focus must be single minded. Nobody starts out with an attitude of defeat. Why compete if you've already decided to settle for the lesser medal? No athlete trains hard for second or third prize.

Olympic athletes have a specific goal, to compete with the best athletes in the world and win. You might not have a goal of being an Olympic athlete, but your goal should be just as important. And Olympic marathon runner has to have incredible endurance and strength in order to compete. Your training should fit your goal. No Olympic athlete sits on the couch all day and eat snacks, drink a 2 liter soda and watch television. These athletes have specific training such as speed work, long runs, and strength and conditioning. Whatever your goal is make sure your training fits. Exercise self-control in your goals. What kind of plan can you execute to get your momentum back? Perhaps you can begin by monitoring your thought life. Think about what you are thinking and take every thought captive. Stop allowing negative thoughts to control your life and bring you down.

Just like an athlete disciplines and trains, so you must discipline your mind to cast down every negative thought of the past and replace it with the word of God.

Replace those negative thoughts with worship and build yourself up in your faith.

Make sure you are digesting a good spiritual diet of prayer, meditation on God's word, and worship. A healthy diet is important for your body to function properly. We often concern ourselves about the food we eat and whether we're eating too much fat or too many calories. An Olympian is concerned about getting the right nutrients and calories to fuel the most important competition in their life. They want to make sure their bodies are performing at its best. You want your mind to perform it's best also. Forgetting the past is all about your mental health. Choose to eliminate all toxic thoughts and negative conversations from your life.

> ***Jude 1:20*** *says, "But you, beloved, building yourselves up on your most holy faith, praying in the Holy Spirit."*

Just like an athlete you must build yourself up. Shadows of the past will bring you down but praying in the Holy Spirit will build you up and edify you. ***Ephesians 6:18*** says,

> *"Pray in the spirit at all times, with every kind of prayer and petition. To this end, stay alert with all perseverance in your prayers for all the saints."*

> *"Let's not neglect the most important plan you can execute in pressing on to your goal - The Armor of God. "Finally be strong in the Lord and in his mighty power. Put on the full armor of God, so that you can take your stand against the devil's schemes.*

> *"For our struggle is not against flesh and blood but against the rulers, against the authorities, against the powers of this dark world and against the spiritual*

SHADOWS OF THE PAST

> *forces of evil in the heavenly realms. Therefore put on the full armor of God, so that when the day of evil comes, you may be able to stand your ground and after you have done everything to stand. Stand firm then, and pray in the Spirit on all occasions with all kinds of prayers and requests."* ***(Ephesians 6:10-20)***

These dark shadows are spiritual forces aligned to stop you from moving forward. Therefore, you must be equipped with the full armor of God to combat the lies and schemes of the devil. Shadows of the past present themselves as reminders to convince you that your past is what's really important. Some people actually believe if they hold on to the memories, it's the only way they can stay connected to the person. No matter how painful, they choose to not let go of the memories. The memories are all they have in holding on to what used to be. In reality the loss represents connection that is broken. Whether it was the loss of a relationship, a divorce or the loss through death. It's time to let go of painful memories and move on. All memories are not unhealthy. You will always love and remember your love ones that passed on into eternity. Time and God will heal that separation. Grieving is a part of the healing process, but you should not grieve forever. You must move on. Do not get trapped in grief; seek counseling and help from a therapist, psychologist, or your pastor. Everyone deals with grief differently. Realize that you are overwhelmed and reach out for help. There are specialists trained to deal with what you are going through.

Shadows of the past can change everything about you.

They can actually turn you into a totally different person. The effects of the past can be life altering. There is usually a change in a person's mood or attitude. There is usually a loss of interest in certain activities they use to enjoy. Many people isolate themselves and withdraw from communicating with friends and family. They become more fatigue and drained of energy. If any of these signs sound like you, seek professional help immediately. You can't get through this alone. If there is a true mental disorder, you will need to get an accurate diagnosis from a mental health doctor in order to know how to proceed.

The most important factor to remember is that you have the victory, and you are more than a conqueror. The Bible contains hundreds of scriptures reminding us that we are victorious. **1Corinthians10:13** says,

> *"No temptation (test) has overtaken you except what is common to mankind. And God is faithful, he will not let you be tempted (tested, tried) beyond what you can bear. But when you are tempted, he will also provide a way out so that you can endure it."*

Don't give up! God has already provided a way out of this test.

> **Ephesians 6:10** *says, "Finally be strong in the Lord and in his mighty power."* **Romans 8:31** *says, "What then shall we say in response to these things? If God is for us, who can be against us? He who did not spare his own son, but gave him up for us all, how will he not also along with him graciously give us all things?"*

1 Corinthians 5:57 *says, "But thanks be to God! He gives us the victory through our Lord Jesus Christ."*

These are just a few of God's promises to remind us that no matter what, we have the victory! Hold your head up! Don't be discouraged! Things are turning around for your good NOW!

5 WHAT IS YOUR PAIN LEVEL FROM 1-10?

Everyone experiences pain differently whether it's mental or physical. Mental pain or mental anguish is very real. So, how do we describe it? The same issue may seem like the worst physical pain ever to one person while someone else may find themselves experiencing only minor pain. To get a better understanding of each individual's pain, there is a simple, yet effective solution created called pain scales. These rating scales provide a way for people to convey to a medical professional what their pain level is. Standard medical pain scales are numeric rating scales that range from 1 to 10 (0 is pain free) with each pain level being increasingly more painful.

For patients, Wong- Baker faces are used for each level 1 through 10 to further access the level of pain they are currently experiencing. Each face corresponds to a specific pain level to give an even better understanding to the patient of which pain level they are at. Zero(0) = pain free, 1 = very minor annoyance or occasional minor twinges, 2= minor annoyances, 3= annoying enough to be distracting, 4 = can be ignored if you are really involved in your work, but still distracting, 5= can't be ignored for more than 30 minutes, 6= can't be ignored for any length of time, but you can still go to work, 7= makes it difficult to concentrate, interferes with sleep but you can still function, 8= physical activity limited, you can read and talk with effort, 9= unable to speak, crying out or moaning uncontrollable, 10 = unconscious pain can make you pass out.

Pain is personal on any level. Communicating this effectively to someone else who isn't experiencing the same pain can be a real challenge. What is even more difficult to describe is mental pain. How do you rate that on a scale? Pain on any level hurts. The good news is there is help for mental illness and mental anguish.

It is not a sign of weakness to lean on God neither is it a sign of weakness to lean on a professional therapist. It is a wise choice to reach out for help. If you were drowning in the lake, would you refuse the help of someone throwing you a life jacket?

If a rescue boat came along, would you turn them away and say, "Thanks but no thanks, I got this?" The answer is of course not! Shadows of the past will drown you. It is critical you understand when you are not coping well in life.

Emotional pain is defined as pain or hurt that originates from non-physical sources. Sometimes this type of pain is the result of the actions of others. Often it is the result of regret, grief, or loss. It is what we call shadows of the past. Emotional pain can also be the result of an underlying mental health condition such as depression or anxiety. It doesn't matter what the cause is, psychological pain can be intense, and it can affect many areas of your life. Although emotional pain is often dismissed as being less serious than physical pain, it is important that it is taken seriously. To dismiss this is like giving a dark shadow permission to follow you throughout your entire life. This affects both your physical and mental health. Various emotions can lead to psychological pain, such as prolonged sadness, unexpressed anger, anxiety, shame and guilt.

Sadness is a natural emotion that is associated with loss or disappointment. However, if it doesn't fade with time, it might point to a more serious condition such as depression. Unexpected anger can also impact your health in a negative way. Anger is actually a basic emotion. It releases adrenaline which increases muscle tension and causes your breathing to increase. This is the "fight" part of the "fight or flight" response.

Anxiety, just like anger, and fear, can also release adrenaline. There is also a "flight" response with anxiety, as well as a feeling of being immobilized or stuck. Shame and guilt can also produce an uneasy and uncomfortable feeling which affects the body as well. There is usually a need to keep something secret, causing stress on the body. Emotional pain can often feel as strong as physical pain, and at times it can cause symptoms of pain throughout the body. Because emotional pain can be so distressing, some people often turn to unhealthy coping mechanisms, such as drugs, smoking, alcohol, overeating and other eating disorders. Although these are referred to as coping mechanisms, they are in reality unhealthy and do not help the person to cope.

There are more healthier ways of coping with emotional pain such as talking to someone you trust, and even exercising. Physical activity has shown to be effective for improving someone's mood. The Bible is full of scriptures that bring encouragement, peace, healing, comfort, and deliverance to every area where you are hurting.

> *"I sought the Lord, and he answered me, he delivered me from all my fears.*
>
> *"Those who look to him are radiant, their faces are never covered with shame.*
>
> *"This poor man called, and the Lord heard him, he saved him out of all his troubles. The anger of the Lord encamps around those who fear him, and he delivers them. Taste and see that the Lord is good, blessed is the one who takes refuge in him. Fear the Lord, you his holy people for those who fear him lack nothing.*
>
> *The eyes of the Lord are on the righteous and his ears are attentive to their cry. The righteous cry out and the Lord hears them; he delivers them from all their troubles. The Lord is close to the brokenhearted and saves those who are crushed in spirit. The righteous person may have many troubles but the Lord delivers him from them all. The Lord will rescue his servant; no one who takes refuge in him will be condemned."* **(Psalm 34 NIV)**

God not only saves us, but he also delivers us and heals us from our afflictions and wounds. We can be made whole physically, spiritually, and emotionally. Heaven never closes.

We can call on God day or night and he will hear us. He delights in answering our prayers and fulfilling every promise he's made. God wants you free from the trauma of your past. He wants to deliver you from haunting memories and dark shadows. Jesus conquered all these things and more in his suffering, his death, burial and resurrection. Colossians 2:15(NIV) says, *"And having disarmed the powers and authorities, he made a public spectacle of them, triumphing over them by the cross."*

> ***2 Corinthians 2:14*** *says, "Now thanks be to God, which always causes us to triumph in Christ, and makes manifest the aroma of his knowledge by us in every place."*

THAT'S LOVE

Jesus was acquainted with sorrow and grief. He experienced every emotion that we experience. He knows what it is like to be lonely and betrayed. He knows what it is like to suffer the loss of a loved one. One of the most graphic depiction of the passion of Christ is found in Isaiah chapter 53. It says :

"He was despised and rejected by mankind, a man of suffering, and familiar with pain. Like one from whom people hide their faces, he was despised and we held him in low esteem." Surely he took up our pain and bore our suffering, yet we considered him punished by God, stricken by him, and afflicted. But he was pierced for our transgressions, he was crushed for our iniquities, the punishment that brought us peace was on him, and by his wounds we were healed.

We all, like sheep have gone astray, each of us has turned to our own way; and the Lord has laid on him the iniquity of us all.

He was oppressed and afflicted; yet he did not open his mouth, he was led like a lamb to the slaughter, and as a sheep before its shearers is silent, so he did not open his mouth.

By oppression and judgment he was taken away. Yet who of his generation protested? For he was cut off from the land of the living; for the transgression of my people he was punished. He was assigned a grave with the wicked; and with the rich in his death; though he had done no violence, nor was any deceit in his mouth.

Yet it was the Lord's will to crush him and cause him to suffer, and though the Lord makes his life an offering for sin, he will see his offspring and prolong his days, and the will of the Lord will prosper in his hand.

After he was suffered, he will see the light of life and be satisfied, by his knowledge my righteous servant will justify many and he will bear their iniquities.

Therefore I will give him a portion among the great and he will divide the spoils with the strong, because he poured out his life unto death, and was numbered with the transgressors. For he bore the sin of many and made intercession for the transgressors."

It is finished! Paid in full! Mission accomplished! There is no excuse remaining for us. Overcoming is your choice. You

WHAT IS YOUR PAIN LEVEL FROM 1 - 10?

can remain a victim of your past or you can become a victor.

You do not have to succumb to shadows of your past. The price that was paid for our freedom is the highest price no one else would dare to pay! Jesus became the ultimate sacrifice. Never again will that price have to be paid. There was a great exchange at the cross. Jesus bound to a cross, not only became sin for us, but he also died as us. His body, which was the veil that was torn, made a way into the Holy of Holies so that we may know him and so we may receive this glorious gift of salvation. *"For Christ did not enter into a holy place made with human hands, which was only a copy of the true one in heaven. He entered into heaven itself to appear now before God on our behalf."* **(Hebrews 9:24 NLT)**

The significance of the Holy of Holies to Christians is found in the events that surround the crucifixion of Christ. When Jesus died, something supernatural and amazing took place. When Jesus died on the cross and cried out "It is finished," something else took place. At that very moment the curtain of the temple was torn in two from top to bottom. **(Matthew 27:50-52)** The veil was not torn in half by any man, but by the power of God to make a resounding statement. Man is no longer separated from God and The New Covenant has been ratified. *"We have confidence to enter the most holy place by the blood of Jesus, by a new and living way opened for us through the curtain, that is, his body."* **(Hebrews 10:19)**

It was necessary for the man of sorrows to suffer. It was the main reason why he came. This was necessary because the penalty for sin against God is death - eternal death, not just physical death. Sin separated us from God, but Jesus Christ's ultimate sacrifice brought us back to God. We owe him our lives- BIG TIME!

NO MORE LAME EXCUSES!

Speaking of lame excuses, there was a man in the Bible who was lame from birth; from his mother's womb, as Luke describes it.

> "One afternoon Peter and John were going to the temple at the hour of prayer, the ninth hour. And a man who was lame from birth was being carried to the temple gate called Beautiful, where he was put every day to beg from those entering the temple courts. When he saw Peter and John about to enter, he asked them for money. Peter looked straight at him, as did John. Then Peter said, Look at us! So the man gave his attention expecting to get something from them. Then Peter said, silver and gold I do not have, but what I do have I give you. In the name of Jesus Christ of Nazareth, Walk! Taking him by the right hand, he helped him up, and instantly the man's feet and ankles became strong. He jumped to his feet and began to walk. Then he went with them into the temple courts, walking and jumping, and praising God. When all the people saw him walking and praising God, they recognized him as the same man who used to sit begging at the temple called Beautiful, and they were filled with wonder and amazement at what had happened to him." **(Acts 3:1-10 NIV)**

WHAT IS YOUR PAIN LEVEL FROM 1 - 10?

This man received a chance at a new life. He didn't get his life back, he never had a real productive life. He got a brand-new life on that day. He was lame from birth. He had never experienced the freedom of walking. He had accepted a life of dependency on others. People brought him to the gate every day so that he could beg for money. Hypothetically, he was not only crippled (lame) in his feet and legs (40 years), but he was also crippled in his mind. He had no hope for a better life because no one presented him with a better life. His support system were people committed to helping him be a beggar for the rest of his life. All that changed instantly! He became a recipient of the grace and mercy of God. He experienced firsthand, the power of the cross! He was healed and given a chance to live a productive life.

You too can be healed today. The same power that raised Jesus from the dead can heal you emotionally and physically. The same power that got the lame man up from his bed, can also raise you up. From that day on, the lame man had no more excuses. It was time for him to move forward and forget his past. No longer would he depend on others to carry him around and take care of him daily. This lame man became self-sufficient in a single day after years of being disabled.

It doesn't matter how long you've struggled in emotional or physical pain. You can be free. You can experience the same joy the "healed" man experienced. He went into the temple walking, jumping and praising God. No longer a beggar, this man joined his community giving glory to God. People labeled him (beggar) based on his past. Now the degrading stereotype had been taken off him and he no longer looked back or went back. Every miracle and every testimony is for the glory of God. This lame man became a living witness of the power of Jesus to heal and deliver.

This seemingly insignificant man that many people overlooked as they went into the temple to pray, is the same man that Peter and John had compassion on. Jesus was always moved with compassion as he preached and healed. Peter and John had the same mark upon their lives. They gave the lame man what money could not buy. They immediately knew that money was not his real need, but wholeness. Many times, we think money is our most important need. We often think, "If I had more money, things would be better and easier, and I would have peace." Real peace is found within you not without. It's not the external factors that bring peace, but inner healing leads to peace and contentment. Peace was often discussed by both Jesus and his apostles.

> ***John 14:27*** *says, "Peace I leave with you, my peace I give to you; not as the world gives do I give to you. Let not your heart be troubled, neither let it be afraid."*

> ***Philippians 4:5-7*** *says, "Do not be anxious about anything, but in every situation, by prayer and petition, with thanksgiving, present your requests to God. And the peace of God, which transcends all understanding will guard your hearts and your minds in Christ Jesus."*

> ***Psalm 29:11*** *says, "The Lord gives strength to his people, the Lord blesses his people with peace."*

Jesus wants you to have peace. He is the Prince of Peace. You are not alone, and neither are you hidden from him. God knew exactly where the lame man was, and he knows where you are. He has the highest, most blessed and prosperous life for you, but you have to let go of the past. You have to see Jesus as being greater than the pain of the past. God knows exactly what to do with the pain and trauma. He wants to erase it from your life and give you a fresh new start in life. Here are instructions from God concerning your past;

> *"Forget the former things, do not dwell on the past. See, I am doing a new thing! Now it springs up; do you not perceive it? I am making a way in the wilderness and streams in the wasteland."* **(Isaiah 43:18)**

Stop excusing yourself from life. Deal with the hand that you've been dealt. Stay in the game and don't you dare fold! Those shadows of the past are only there to bluff you. Little do you know; you have the winning hand.

SHADOWS OF THE PAST

6 I HAVE ISSUES

I have issues, you have issues. All God's children have issues. There is an expression that is often said, "You have issues." What does that actually mean? Well, it depends on the situation. It is without a doubt a very cultural, sometimes urban slang word. Issues can be related to mental or psychological disorders that make it very difficult to continue a relationship. Issues can also be a callous way of ending a relationship or a date. Having issues may have behavioral tendencies for a variety of reasons. Most likely the issues are a result of negative life experiences. Usually, people with issues may be very negative or defensive most of the time. They may repeatedly involve themselves in bad relationships because they have issues from the past. To say a person has issues is basically saying there is something wrong with them. In "slang" terms, having issues implies the state of one's mind, as in "crazy," a "little off," and "not all together there," or "the elevator doesn't go all the way to the top floor." However, having issues are real. Many issues arise from relationship problems. Some of the most common issues people have in relationships are: communication, growing apart, infidelity, traumas, not feeling appreciated, money, parenting, and rejection. Issues arise when it becomes difficult to resolve conflicts and situations. No matter how nice you are, conflict and offense are certain to arise. We don't live on an island by ourselves; therefore disagreements can become issues. Dealing with people that have issues of the past is challenging, to say the least. Some people are entrenched in their past. They believe what they believe and there is no convincing them otherwise. You are not called to solve every issue. Someone else's issue does not have to become yours. Concentrate on your own issues and find a way to work through them. Things change, and so do issues. They are not permanent. Life experiences can change you for the best or the worst. You decide whether or not your past will control your life. It's time to focus on the present, not the past. Having issues are not based on a particular class or race of people. Relationship issues go back as far as the creation. In the book of Genesis, Cain and Abel are the first two sons of Adam and Eve. Cain, the firstborn was a farmer, and his brother Abel was a shepherd. Both brothers made a sacrifice and brought it before God, each of his own produce and animal. God favored Abel's sacrifice instead of Cain's. Issues of jealousy and anger arose because of this, and Cain murdered Abel. Cain's punishment from God was a sentence to a life of wandering. (Genesis 4:1-16) Let's take a look at all the emotions running in this story.

> *"Why are you so angry?" The Lord asked why do you look so dejected? You will be accepted if you do what is right. But if you refuse to do what is right, then watch out! Sin is crouching at the door, eager to control you. But you must subdue it and be its master. One day Cain suggested to his brother, let's go out into the fields. And while they were in the field, Cain attacked his brother,*

Abel, and killed him. Afterward the Lord asked Cain, where is your brother? Where is Abel? I don't know Cain responded. Am I my brother's guardian? But the Lord said, what have you done? Listen! Your brothers blood cries out to me from the ground. Now you are cursed and banished from the ground, which has swallowed your brother's blood. No longer will the ground yield good crops for you, no matter how hard you work! From now on you will be a homeless wanderer on the earth. Cain replied to the Lord, My punishment is too great for me to bear. You have banished me from the land and from your presence, you have made me a homeless wanderer. Anyone who finds me will kill me! The Lord replied, no for I will give a seven fold punishment to anyone who kills you. Then the Lord put a mark on Cain to warn anyone who might try to kill him. So Cain left the Lord's presence and settled in the land of nod east of Eden." **(Genesis 4:6-16)**

There are a lot of issues going on in the story. You think you got issues? Think again. What a dysfunctional family this was! After Adam and Eve sinned and became separated from God, they had two sons Cain and Abel. This passage details the murder of Abel by his older brother Cain, the first son of Adam and Eve. Cain worked the ground and Abel tended sheep. They both worshipped God, bringing an offering to the Lord. Cain kills Abel in a fit of envy and rage over God's rejection of his offering. The fact is, he did not bring God his best. *"At harvest time Cain brought to the Lord a "gift" (the keyword of his farm produce)."* (verse 3) While Abel brought several choice lambs from the best of his flock. (verse 4) The Lord accepted

Abel and his offering." The first human born on the earth became the first murderer. We're talking about dark shadows of the past. This would forever follow Cain for the rest of his life. The consequences of sin became apparent in Chapter 4. Envy, rage, arrogance, rebellion, murder, punishment, separation from family and separation from God was his portion in life. These are serious issues. Adam and Eve's first-born son Cain, in jealousy murders his brother Abel and loses everything. In the end, Adam and Eve lost them both, one to a murderous act and the other to being banished. Anyone's past can be full of dark shadows of regret, sin, murder, guilt and shame. Please understand, we all have to pay a price for the decisions and choices we make. You will not escape some kind of punishment for your actions. God is merciful and full of grace. He is forgiving and long-suffering, but there is a time of sowing from those bad seeds of sin, disobedience, and rebellion. Sowing and reaping is a divine principle. When we sow good seeds, we reap a good harvest. When we so bad seeds, we reap a bad harvest. It's very simple. God loves you and he will still bless you, but you "pluck up" what you "put down." The seed is never confused. You plant apple seeds, and you reap apples. Don't get it twisted! You're not reaping lettuce. Again, you reap what you sow! Methods are many, principles are a few. Methods will change, but principles never do. Remember this little rhyming phrase and you will always know that the principal will never change. There will always be memories of the past, but they don't have to keep you from living your best life. In spite of being banished, Cain went on to having a wife and family of his own. He became the founder of the city Enoch, which was named after his son. No matter how shady your past is, you can move on and learn from your mistakes.

THE BORN IDENTITY

Will the real Esau step forward! This story that we are about to examine is full of twists and turns. It is full of issues and conflicts. It is full of lies and deception, and it is full of reconciliation. These chapters in the book of **Genesis (25-33)** read like a drama story made for a big screen movie production. These twin boys were at odds from the very beginning. Their intrauterine interaction was very unusual, giving us a glimpse of what would occur as they became older. Jacob came out at birth grabbing Esau's heel, unconsciously denoting, "Don't you dare try to come first!" Or "Get back here, not so fast!" The babies had no comprehension that according to the Hebrew culture, the firstborn child gets a bigger inheritance, the birthright inheritance., hence receiving a special anointing placed upon his life. These twins were contending for the first-born birthright blessing even in the womb. **Genesis 25:22** says

> *"The babies jostled each other within her, and she said, Why is this happening to me? So she went to inquire of the Lord. And the Lord said to her, two nations are in your womb, and two people from within you will be separated; one people will be stronger than the other, and the older will serve the younger. Jacob's name in Hebrew means "trickster," and Esau's name means "hairy." "When the time*

> came for her to give birth, there were twin boys in her womb. The first to come out was red, and his whole body was like a hairy garment, so they named him Esau. After this, his brother came out, with his hand grasping Esau's heel so he was named Jacob."

Genesis 25:24-26 The struggle began to intensify as they became older. Jacob, along with his mother Rebecca conspired to steal Esau's birthright.

> "The boys grew up, and Esau became a skillful hunter, a man of the open country, while Jacob was content to stay at home among the tents. Isaac who had a taste for wild game, loved Esau but Rebecca loved Jacob. Once when Jacob was cooking some stew, Esau came in from the open country famished. He said to Jacob, "Quick, let me have some of that red stew! I am famished! (That is why he was also called Edom). Jacob replied, First sell me your birthright. Look, I am about to die he said, What good is the birthright to me? But Jacob said, Swear to me first. So he swore an oath to him, selling his birthright to Jacob. Then Jacob gave Esau some bread and some lentil stew. He ate and drank and then got up and left. So, Esau despised his birthright." **(Genesis 25:29-34)**

Can't you just see the story on the movie screen? We see the trickster Jacob doing his thing! He's the best con artist ever. Clearly, he coveted Esau's birthright from the very beginning. It appears he was just waiting for the perfect opportunity to nab that birthright. The clever thing about it is that it is cunning but legal. You really can't classify it as theft.

I HAVE ISSUES

There was an exchange here of goods and service. Now we could argue the point that he Esau was coerced into giving up his birthright. The fact is, no pressure was applied to Esau. He was famished and was willing to give up his birthright. Well you know the saying, *"A person will do anything, when they are hungry."* Esau was at the point of starvation and he sold the most valuable thing he possessed - his birthright. The next pivotal scene occurs when Jacob steals Esau's blessing. **(Genesis 27)**

Not only did Jacob steal his birthright, but he also stole his blessing that their father Isaac would bestow upon him before he died. Here's identity theft at its best! We're talking about big time sibling rivalry! We see this unfold in one of the most painful narratives of scripture. This is so emotional! Isaac wants to bless his favorite son, but Rebecca convinces her favorite son, Jacob, to steal the blessing. Can you believe that? Such family drama is playing out like a movie.

> *"Now Rebecca was listening as Isaac spoke to his son Esau. When Esau left for the open country to hunt game and bring it back, Rebecca said to her son Jacob, Look, I overheard your father say to your brother Esau, bring me some game and prepare me some tasty food to eat, so that I may give you my blessing in the presence of the Lord before I die. Now, my son, listen carefully and do what I tell you. Go out to the flock and bring me two choice young goats, so I can prepare some tasty food for your father, just the way he likes it. Then take it to your father to eat, so that he may give you his blessing before he dies. Jacob said to Rebecca his*

mother, but my brother Esau is a hairy man while I have smooth skin. What if my father touches me? I would appear to be tricking him and would bring down a curse on myself rather than a blessing." **(Genesis 27:5-12)**

Jacob knew the repercussions of this whole devious plan. He said, "I would appear to be tricking him." This is not only "trickery" but deception. Jacob of course you're tricking your father! He also knew the consequences of his actions would be a curse placed upon him. Let's continue: *"His mother said to him, my son let the curse fall on me. Just do what I say, go and get them for me (versus 13.).* A mother is a mother is a mother. There is no limit to what a mother will do for her child. She will walk barefoot through life for her child. In this case, she will take a curse upon herself just to see her favorite child gain the advantage and the blessing for the rest of his life.

"Then Rebecca took the best clothes of Esau her older son, which she had in the house, and put them on her younger son Jacob. She also covered his hands and the smooth part of his neck with the goat skins. Then she handed to her son Jacob the tasty food and the bread she had made. He went to his father and said, My father. Yes, my son, he answered who is it? Jacob said to his father, I am Esau your firstborn. I have done as you told me. Please sit up and eat some of my game, so that you may give me your blessing. Isaac asked his son, how did you find it so quickly, my son? The Lord your God gave me success, he replied. Then Isaac said to Jacob, Come near so I can touch you, my son, to know whether you really are my son

I HAVE ISSUES

Esau or not. Jacob went close to his father Isaac, who touched him and said, The voice is the voice of Jacob, but the hands are the hands of Esau. He did not recognize him, for his hands were hairy like those of his brother Esau, so he proceeded to bless him. Are you really my son Esau? He asked. I am, he replied."

HOOK, LINE, AND SINKER

As you continue to read the story, you see that Isaac was old and his eyes became dim. He was also very cautious and careful about releasing that blessing. He was a little skeptical about the identity of Esau, because the voice of Jacob caused him to be reluctant. Although he felt like Esau, he did not sound like Esau, and he did not smell like Esau. Here is what you need to understand about the pronunciation of a blessing. Blessings once pronounced are established. The only one that can revoke a blessing is God. Even those pronouncing the blessing cannot revoke them. A spoken blessing over someone invokes the blessing of God in their lives. Therefore when God pronounces the blessing upon you, it cannot be reversed. You are blessed!"

"Then Isaac said, now my son, bring me the wild game. Let me eat it, and then I will give you my blessing. So Jacob took the food to his father and Isaac ate it. He also drank the wine that Jacob served him. Then Isaac said to Jacob, please come a little closer and kiss me my son. So Jacob went over and kissed him. And when Isaac caught the smell of his clothes, he was finally convinced, and he blessed his son. He said, Ah! The smell of my son is like the

smell of the outdoors, which the Lord has dressed!"

THE BLESSING

"From the dew of heaven and the richness of the earth, may God always give you abundant harvest of grain and bountiful new wine. May many nations become your servants, and may they bow down to you. May you be the master over your brothers, and may your mother's sons bow down to you. All who curse you will be cursed, all who bless you will be blessed. As soon as Isaac had finished blessing Jacob and almost before Jacob had left his father, Esau prepared a delicious meal and brought it to his father. Then he said, Sit up my father, and eat my wild game so you can give me your blessing. But Isaac asked him, who are you? Esau replied, It's your son, your firstborn son Esau? Isaac began to tremble uncontrollably and said, Then who just served me with wild game? I have already eaten it, and I blessed him just before you came. And yes, that blessing must stand! When Esau heard his father's word, he let out a loud and bitter cry. Oh my father, what about me? Bless me too! He begged." " But Isaac said, Your brother was here, and he tricked me. He has taken away your blessing. Esau exclaimed, No wonder his name is Jacob, for now he has cheated me twice. First he took my rights as the firstborn, and now he has stolen my blessing. Oh, haven't you saved even one blessing for me? Isaac said to Esau, I have made Jacob your master and have declared that all his brothers will be his servants. I have guaranteed him an abundance of grain and wine . What is left for me to give you, my son?

Esau pleaded, But do you not have only one blessing? Oh my father bless me too! Then Esau broke down and wept. Finally, his father Isaac said to him, You will live away from the richness of the earth, and away from the dew of the heaven above. You will live by your sword and you will serve your brother. But when you decide to break free, you will shake his yoke from your neck.

It is imperative that you take note to this last statement. *"But when you decide to break free..."* YOU can stop the madness of the past in your life. YOU can break free from the shadows of the past and move forward. YOU can shake that yoke of pain, bitterness, disappointment, betrayal, guilt, shame, rejection, and loss off your neck. But the key is, you have to decide. The story of Esau crying and begging his father for just one more blessing is heart wrenching. There is such hurt and despair in Esau's words. After Jacob steals his brother's blessing, he runs away from home at the advice of his mother, because Esau wanted to kill him. According to Genesis 26:23 Isaac and his family had settled in Beersheba, which was near the southern border of Judah. So when Jacob fled he went from Beersheba all the way to Haran which is where his mother Rebecca came from. He spent the next 20 years there. Little did he know that his trickery would turn into two decades of hard labor. The "trickster" (Jacob) got tricked and the "conman" (Jacob) got conned. His father-in-law tricked him into marrying Leah after seven years of hard labor, when he wanted to marry Rachel. Hence, he had to work another seven years. Then for an additional six years he worked for his father-in-law, while his wages were reduced ten times. Talk about learning a lesson, Jacob reaped what he sowed. Twenty years later, God tells him to return to his homeland, which was all the way back to the southern border of Canaan. Somehow, he learned that his brother Esau lived in a neighboring region. Jacob became nervous and afraid, so he sent out scouts to assess the situation. However, he caught wind of his brothers return and started pursuing him. *Jacob's scouts came back and said, "We went to your brother Esau, and now he's coming to meet you, and four hundred men are with him."* **(Genesis 32:6)** Jacob develops a defense strategy to meet his brother. He plays it safe just in case his brother still wants revenge. In the meantime, at night Jacob has a God- encounter. He wrestles with an angel refusing to let him go until he (the angel) bless him. Miraculously Jacob prevailed. Then God says to him (message paraphrase) "Your name is no longer Jacob, From now on it is Israel." Jacob received an identity change. This change affected the history of the world because Jacob became Israel and Israel became a nation that fulfilled God's promise to Abraham, Isaac, and now Jacob. After all the issues of Jacob and Esau's past, they were reconciled. *"But Esau ran to meet Jacob and embraced him. He threw his arms around his neck and kissed him, and they wept."* **(Genesis 33:4)** What kind of man had Esau become that he could forgive like this? We know Jacob's story of being humbled and transformed but the last time we saw Esau, he wanted to kill Jacob. Now, he runs and kisses him and weeps with him. Only God can turn such a horrible past into a victorious future. We don't understand how God does it, but he can reach way down deep into the depths of our hearts and change us. He can heal every soul wound and every emotional wound. Allow God to settle every issue of the past in your life, just as he did with Jacob and Esau. Over the years, they both accumulated extreme wealth and didn't want for anything because God had blessed them. But what they lacked was reconciliation and healing. Your greatest need might not be money, but peace. So, right now we pronounce the blessing upon you:

> *"The Lord bless you and keep you; the Lord make his face to shine upon you and be gracious to you, The Lord lift up his countenance upon you and give you peace."* **(Numbers 6:24-26)**

SHADOWS OF THE PAST

7 CTRL + ALT + DEL

(Control+ Alt + Delete)

Ctrl +Alt + Delete is a computer keyboard command on IBM PC compatible computers, invoked by pressing the delete key while holding the control and Alt keys. This is usually done to interrupt or facilitate interrupting a function. **CTRL + Alt + Delete** keys are used simultaneously in order to close or terminate an application that is not responding, reboot the computer, log in, and proceed. There are also other computer terminology such as spam, junk mail, and shift that are vital functions.

This is somewhat of a lesson in computer 101. However, there is a correlation between those key functions, computer terminology and life. Learning how to use these key functions allows you to get the most out of your computer. We often experience certain interruptions in our emails. At the core of our emails are spam and junk mail that clutter our inbox. While junk mail often comes from opt in services, such as from businesses, spam refers to messages that the user did not opt to receive. While everyone thinks of email when they hear the word "spam," it fits a broader definition.

In addition to the spam messages, you get in your email, you can also receive spam messages via text, in an instant message, and even as comments on websites. Spam is literally invading our lives. Many cell phone carriers have attempted to aid us in filtering out unsolicited business calls by alerting us when the call is coming in. There is a "scam likely" notification that appears and you can ignore the call or delete the call. Spam can also be irrelevant or inappropriate messages sent on the Internet to a large number of people. It is basically linked with hitting a lot of people with the same unsolicited message.

Junk mail is always in the form of mail, or email. It can be unsolicited advertising or promotional material. Both spam and junk mail can contain malware designed to damage your computer or mobile device, or to steal your personal information. They can also be phishing attempts to steal sensitive information from you.

We just laid the basis for this chapter, Ctrl +Alt + Del. We gave you a little refresher on the basic knowledge of keyboarding and computers. The control (Ctrl) key is a modifier key which when pressed in conjunction with another key, performs a special operation, similar to the "Shift" key. The Control (Ctrl) key rarely performs any function when pressed by itself. The Alternate (Alt) key is used to change (alternate) the function of other pressed keys. Hence, the Alt key is a modifier key used in a similar fashion to the shift key.

The Delete (Del) key is typically used to delete either the character ahead of or beneath either the cursor, or the currently selected object. This key is sometimes referred to as the "forward delete" key. Now, let's parallel our lives with these basic functions.

CONTROL (CTRL)

Control means to make decisions about how something is managed or done. Control is the power to direct the actions of someone or something. Here are some common synonyms of control: authority, command, dominion, jurisdiction, power, and sway. While all these words mean "the right to govern or rule or determine, control stresses the power to direct and restrain. Here are some characteristics of control:

- Forward-looking
- Continuous activity
- Managerial function
- Planning
- Action
- Decision making

Life is all about control. It is about taking action and shifting when necessary. It is also about making critical decisions for your future. Choosing to leave the past behind and move forward is the beginning of change. Life can be overwhelming. Many people feel stuck in a rut. They don't know how or where to begin to move forward. The pace of life is accelerating so fast until it's hard to keep up. Anxiety is also at an all-time high creating fear of how one is going to maintain their quality of living. It's time to call a "time out." Regroup and get back in a position of control. It's time to "shift." It's time to regain power over your life.

Your emotions and your beliefs drive your thinking, and your thinking drives your actions. We are a product of what we think. It is vital that we make a mental shift immediately. The Bible says in **Proverbs 23:7**, *"For as he thinketh in his heart ,so is he."* Have you ever heard the expression "You are what you eat?" In a nutritional sense, there is a lot of truth to that statement. In the Scriptures it seems to suggest a different truth; we are what we think. "For as he thinketh in his heart, so is he."

There is a strong desire in most people to maximize their potential and to do well in life. The Bible speaks about the power of the mind and our thoughts. Our minds are powerful and our thoughts shape who we are and who we will become. Control your thoughts and you will control your life.

> *"Do not copy the behavior and customs of this world, but let God transform you into a new person by changing the way you think. Then you will learn to know God's will for you, which is good and pleasing and perfect* **(Romans 12:2)**

The Bible is the best and most relevant self-help book ever. Although written centuries ago, it remains more up to date than the latest breaking news story. There is life, love, and liberty in the word of God. It's power transcends into every generation, culture, and people. The word of God's power is limitless. According to the word of God, you can become a new person if you allow God to change the way you think. Having control over your life is having power.

Changing the way you think changes your perspective on life and the past. You are then able to put the past in "junk mail" or consider it "spam." The shadows of your past get filed away where they rightfully belong in trash. Remember, all unsolicited emails or text messages are considered junk mail or spam. You didn't ask for depression, so move it out of your life. You didn't ask for guilt, shame, rejection and discouragement. Don't hesitate to eliminate it from your life. *"God has not given us a spirit of fear and timidity, but of power, love, and self-discipline."* **(2 Timothy 1:7)**

We can control the negative thoughts in our mind that keep us lingering in the past and stops us from moving forward. **2 Corinthians 10:5** says; *"We demolish arguments and every pretension that sets itself up against the knowledge of God, and we take captive every thought to make it obedient to Christ."* The Apostle says, we take captive. We arrest and subdue every thought; we bring it into subjection causing it to be submissive to the will of God. We don't play around with this. We demolish it, tear it down and pluck it up by the root. What you choose to see determines your reality. You have the power to change your reality by shifting your focus off the past. This is how you shift your life and take control.

ALTERNATE (ALT)

This key on the computer keyboard is used to change (alternate) the function of other pressed keys. Hence, the Alt key is a modifier key used in a similar fashion to the shift key. Once again, it's time to shift your life. It's time to modify certain areas in your life. Let's start by pinpointing areas that are not congruent with the will of God. To alternate means to interchange repeatedly and regularly. An alternate plan or method is one that you can use if you do not want to use another one. Alternative is choosing between one or more possibilities. These words are quite similar but different. Alternate means an action of "switching" or shifting while alternative is another word for "choice" or option.

Let's concentrate on both, shifting and choosing. There is deliberate action involved in both. You have to choose between living in the past or shifting to a new and better future. You can't do both. Life is all about choices and having options. We are faced with choices every day. Some are small insignificant choices like, "What am I going to eat today?" There are other choices we must make that are big, significant and life-changing. Whether big or small, choices have to be made. Living in the shadows of the past is a choice. Breaking free and moving forward is a choice. Choosing to be blessed is a choice. It's all about Ctrl + Alt (control and alternate). Unfortunately, life doesn't have a keyboard that we can hit or shift. It's not that simple. There are choices we have to make and an action we have to take.

God created us with a "free will" to make our own choices, therefore, ultimately we are responsible for our future and our actions. Undoubtably, the choice that had the biggest consequence in history took place in the garden of Eden. Eve was deceived into sinning while Adam chose to sin despite knowing what God said.

"The woman said to the serpent, we may eat fruit from the trees in the garden, but God did say, You must not eat fruit from the tree that is in the middle of the garden, and you must not touch it, or you will die. You will not certainly die, the serpent said to the woman. Here is Deception! When the woman saw that the fruit of the tree was good for food and pleasing to the eye, and also desirable for gaining wisdom, she took some and ate it. She also gave some to her husband, who was with her, and he ate it.

And God said, Who told you that you were naked? "Have you eaten from the tree that I commanded you not to eat from?" The man said, The woman you put here with me she gave me some fruit from the tree, and I ate it. Then the Lord God said to the woman, What is this you have done? The woman said, The serpent deceived me, and I ate." **(Genesis chapter 3)**

Here is a classic illustration of not taking responsibility for our choices and actions. We find it easier to blame others for our misfortunes and mistakes in life. Someone else is always a reason why we can't do any better or why we can't get ahead in life. It's all about playing the "blame" game. You hear people say things like, "If it wasn't for what happened to me as a child, I would not have all these problems" or "If it wasn't for the emotional pain he (she) took me through in the relationship, I wouldn't have all these trust issues." The "blame game" goes back as far as Adam and Eve. Adam blamed Eve for giving him the fruit while Eve blamed the serpent for deceiving her. Actually Adam blamed God as well for choosing Eve for him. The moral of the story is they all paid a price for the choices they made and they suffered the consequences, including the serpent.

All of us have made choices in our lives that resulted in consequences; some good and some bad. Given the opportunity again, we would probably make different choices because we learn from those mistakes. We are supposed to become wiser from our past choices. The Bible is our life manual for everything we experience in life. Romans 15:4 says,

> "For everything that was written in the past was written to teach us, so that through the endurance taught in the Scriptures and the encouragement they provide we might have hope."

Remember, Ctrl + Alt. Be willing to admit mistakes and adjust (alternate) accordingly. There is no wisdom in continuing down the wrong path after you have discovered it is wrong. You must be willing to shift, modify, and alternate.

DELETE

The delete key on most computer keyboards, which is typically used to delete either (in text mode), the character ahead of or beneath the cursor over the currently selected object. In general, delete or remove refers to the act of eliminating a file, text, or another object from the computer hard drive. In Microsoft windows, deleted files are sent to the Recycle Bin. On Apple computers, deleted files are sent to the Trash.

How wonderful is that! You have the power to delete. Nothing in your past, present, or future is written in stone. You can eliminate all the negative vibes out of your life. You can delete shadows of the past whenever you choose to do so. Another word for delete is erase. You can't erase the memories of the past, but you can erase the pain and suffering. The word delete also means to strike or remove, cancel and expunge. It means to destroy something, blot it out and cut it off.

You must make it a priority to delete that which is negative from your life. Assess where you are in life, and where you want to be. Then decide what it will take for you to be on a new level. What we are saying is, add up the cost. Be ready to put the time in for your next level, because it's going to cost you something. Be ready to delete some people, places, things, habits, and behavior. That's why computers have "delete" keys. Why sit and wish to change the memo or text when you have the capability of changing it by deleting it before you send it. Count the cost first. Jesus gave the disciples instructions on what it means to "count the cost."

> *"For which of you desiring to build a tower, does not first sit down and count the cost, whether he has enough to complete it? Otherwise, when he has laid a foundation and is not able to finish, all who see it begin to mock him, saying, This man began to build and was not able to finish. Or what king going out to encounter another king in war will not sit down first and deliberate whether he is able with 10,000 to meet him who comes against him with 20,000?*

> *And if not, while the other is yet a great way off, he sends a delegation and asks for terms of peace. So therefore, anyone of you that does not renounce all that he has cannot be my disciple. "* **(Luke 14:26-33)**

Clearly, in life, there are things we have to give up in order to follow Christ. But we must also count the cost of having peace, prosperity, and success. Assess the cost first. Figure out what you have to "add" to your life and what you must "delete" from your life. After deleting the negative, it is for certain you want to add these things in order to succeed in life:

> *"For this very reason, make every effort to supplement your faith with virtue, and virtue knowledge, and knowledge with self-control, and self-control with steadfastness, and steadfastness with godliness, and godliness with brotherly affection, and brotherly affection with love. For if these qualities are yours and are increasing, they keep you from being ineffective or unfruitful in the knowledge of our Lord Jesus Christ. For whoever lacks these qualities is so nearsighted that he is blind, having forgotten that he was cleansed from his former sins. For if you practice these qualities, you will never fail."* **(2 Peter 1:3-11 ESV)**

This is your recipe for success and living your best prosperous life.

8 LETTING GO

In this chapter we want to specifically deal with "trauma." What is trauma? We all have our own idea of what we think trauma is. Let's accurately define it. Trauma is an "emotional response" to a terrible event like rape, an accident, or even a natural disaster. Immediately after the event, shock and denial are typical responses. There are usually longer-term reactions such as flashbacks, relationship issues, emotional outburst, and even physical symptoms such as headaches.

Trauma symptoms can affect many areas of your life. You can be traumatized and not even recognize it as a trauma. Witnessing an accident or witnessing the death of a loved one can traumatize you. Some people are traumatized by living in an unsafe neighborhood and watching crime escalate, feeling rejected by a parent and or medical condition. Being involved in a relationship with a physically abusive person can cause trauma. Providing care for a parent can traumatize you. There are so many things in life that can traumatize you.

It is important to pinpoint these areas of trauma that have occurred and properly deal with them. Pretending to be "OK" is not "OK." Perhaps reading this chapter will even strike a nerve in you and make you feel uncomfortable. You might even have a flashback while reading this. You won't be alone.

We've all experienced trauma at some point in our lives. Life has a way of coming at you, and it's not always easy to just roll with the punches or go with the flow. There is a saying, "Just relax, things will work themselves out." Whoever said that must've been seriously misguided. Things don't just "Work themselves out." You have to become a part of the process of healing and deliverance. Saying things will work themselves out, is like telling the airplane pilot, "Relax take a seat, the plane will fly on his own and whatever it lands will be fine." This sounds absurd, doesn't it? It is just as absurd to ignore the trauma that you've experienced. Truthfully you are probably still experiencing the trauma.

People respond differently to bad things that happen and overwhelm them. Trauma is your response to the distressing event that you realize is difficult to cope with. A World Mental Health survey conducted by the World Health Organization found that at least a third of the more than 125,000 people surveyed in 26 different countries had experienced trauma. That number rose to 70% when the group was limited to people experiencing core disorders as defined by the Diagnostic and Statistical Manuel of Mental Disorders, 4th Edition (DSM- IV). However, these numbers are just report numbers. The actual number is probably much higher. These are staggering enough.

It's hard to tell which events will cause post traumatic symptoms, but circumstances typically involve loss of control, betrayal, abuse of power, pain, confusion, helplessness, war, and natural disaster. Traumatic situations that cause post traumatic symptoms may vary from person to person. Not every traumatized person develops post-traumatic stress disorder (PTSD). Here is one thing to remember, when the symptoms last more than a month and seriously affect your ability to function, you may be suffering from PTSD. The symptoms are not always immediate. Some people don't show symptoms until months after the event. PTSD can be very debilitating with panic attacks, depression, suicidal thoughts and feelings, drug abuse, insomnia, feelings of being isolated and not being able to complete everyday tasks.

When we look at some of the characters in the Bible, we find that people during that time are not different from people now. Of course, we are in a technological explosion age and life is 1,000 times better because of technological advancements in science, medicine, electronics, arts, and entertainment etc. People had serious issues back then too. They had traumatic events that occurred all the time. King David went to war often and many of them probably suffered from PTSD though it wasn't diagnosed at that time. In one account in 1 Samuel 30, David and his men were definitely traumatized when they returned from battle to the city of Ziklag and found the city had been burned with fire by the Amalekites. Their wives and children were also taken captive. David's men were so traumatized and cried until they had no strength. They were so distraught at their loss that they spoke of stoning David to death. The men the Bible says were bitter in their soul. Even David himself was greatly distressed. Who knows, Moses and the children of Israel had to be traumatized as Pharaoh and his army chased them right to the Red Sea! What were they going to do? It was too much water to swim. If that doesn't traumatize you, I don't know what will. Honestly, they probably had flashbacks of that event for years. Let's take a look.

ISRAEL'S S.O.S.

"When the Israelites saw the king and his army marching against them, they were terrified and cried out to the Lord for help. They said to Moses, Weren't there any graves in Egypt? Did you bring us out here in the desert to die? Look what you have done by bringing us out of Egypt. Didn't we tell you before we left that this would happen? We told you to leave us alone and let us go on being slaves of the Egyptians. It would be better to be slaves there than to die here in the desert. Moses answered, don't be afraid! Stand your ground, and you will see what the Lord will do to save you today. You will never see these Egyptians again. The Lord will fight for you and all you have to do is keep still." "The Lord said to Moses, why are you crying out for help? Tell the people to move forward. Lift up your walking stick and hold it over the sea. The water will divide and the Israelites will be able to walk through the sea on dry ground. I will make the Egyptians so stubborn that they will go in after them, and I will gain honor by my victory over the king, his army, his chariot, and his drivers. When I defeat them, the Egyptians will know that I am the Lord." "Moses held out his hand over the sea, and the Lord drove the sea back with a strong east wind. It blew all night and turned the sea into dryland. The water *was divided and the Israelites walked through the sea into dry ground, with walls of water on both sides. The Egyptians pursued them and went after them into the sea with all the horses, chariots and drivers. The Egyptians said, The Lord is fighting for the Israelites against us. Let's get out of here! On that day the Lord saved the people of Israel from the Egyptians and the Israelites saw them lying dead on the seashore. When the Israelites saw the great power with which the Lord had defeated the Egyptians, they stood in awe of the Lord and they had faith in the Lord and in his servant Moses."* **(Genesis Chapter 14 GNT)**

This is one of the most exciting stories in the Bible. It is also one of the most famous stories made into a big screen movie - **"The Ten Commandments."** What a grand depiction of Moses (actor Charleston Heston) parting the Red Sea with his staff, along with millions of Israelites going into the sea on dry land. However, this is more than an Oscar award winning movie. It was the real deal. This miracle of parting the Red Sea actually happened. Furthermore the impact of this event was traumatizing to say the least. Take note to the emotions that are mentioned in the Scriptures: "They were terrified," "They cried out to the Lord for help," "Did you bring us out here in the desert to die?" "Moses answered don't be afraid." The Lord said to Moses, "Why are you crying for help? This is traumatic! They are scared out of their minds. This is fear on another level. They are afraid and angry. This is swim or die time, and they just knew this would certainly be death by drowning. **But God Always Keeps His Promises!** He promised their ancestors that he would deliver them out of Egypt, and he did just that.

The point of this Bible story is to show you that anyone, at any time, and any place can experience a traumatic event. There is comfort in the word of God. When you become overwhelmed with trying to figure life out, you can always go to the word of God.

LET GO AND LET GOD

There has to be a time of letting go of the trauma from the past. We must face the fact that we are fragile, and we can get overloaded with the cares of this life. As strong as you might be in your own eyes and in the eyes of others, you are not God. You were not made to bear every burden. You are not a beast of burden. You feel pain and you can be broken. The good news is there is help. There are many ways of letting go of trauma. You can't erase the events of the past, but you can deal with your response to the traumatic events. There is healing and deliverance from the shadows of trauma.

> *In **1 Peter 5:6-7** we are instructed; "Humble yourselves, therefore, under God's mighty hand that he may lift you up in due time. Cast all your anxiety (care) on him because he cares for you."*

We are commanded to humble ourselves in light of who God is. He is God, and we are not. Part of humbling ourselves is acknowledging our need for help. As humans, we find it hard to let go of things that so deeply hurt us. We often overestimate our ability to handle situations. God is all-powerful, all-knowing and he is able to handle all our cares, past, present, and future. To "cast" literally means to throw. It is from the Greek word used to describe how the people threw their coats on the colt before Jesus rode into Jerusalem on Palm Sunday *(Luke 19:35)*. In the same way, we should not hold onto our cares. Instead, we should let them go; throw them on our father God who cares for us. His shoulders are big enough to carry all of your traumatic situations. Cares refer to worries, difficulties, and anxieties. Whatever weighing you down should be given to God. Jesus also invited people to come to him, all who were weary and burdened, and he promised to give them rest. *(Matthew 11:28–30)*

Casting your cares on God means that you no longer have to drag behind your dark shadows of painful events. Feelings of pain, rejection, lack of self-worth and despair are felt by most people at some point in life. It's time to let go and let God. Letting go is not a sign of weakness but strength. Letting go is acknowledging you need help that is greater than yourself.

Trauma is deep rooted and can affect every area of your life. Along with casting your cares on God, you may also seek help from a mental health professional, a psychologist or therapist. It's important that you find someone you can talk to and lean on. Let those that are close to you know you are struggling. Too often, those who are going through traumatic issues suffer in silence until it's too late. Your mental health is worth it's weight in gold. Recovery is not always immediate, sometimes it happens little by little, so be patient with yourself and don't give up. Depending on the severity of the trauma and your mental state, it can take months or even years to feel normal again. Don't be afraid to choose therapy. You can trust God and use therapy. That does not make you less spiritual. Therapy is the best option for many that struggle with PTSD and depression. The methods they use are backed by medical studies. Another plus to having a therapist or counselor is they can get to know you and help you by tailoring a specific treatment plan that will be the best based on your traumatic experiences.

In this chapter we have given you many tools to help you heal. **Joshua 1:9** is your personal word from God. *"Have I not commanded you? Be strong and courageous. Do not be afraid, do not be discouraged, for the Lord your God will be with you wherever you go."* God's got you!

9 FANNING THE FLAMES

LET THE FIRE GO OUT

The term *"fanning the flames"* has a couple of implications. Literally speaking, this idiom or metaphor means to blow air (oxygen) on to the fire to increase the intensity of the flames. If you want the fire to continue; you must fan it. Just as the wind makes forest fires worse, so fanning makes the fire intensify. The wind can be an enemy to brushfires. You would think the opposite would be true, fanning a flame does not make it go out. The terminology was used by Dickens in the mid - 1800's in the Old Curiosity Shop.

Fanning the flames in the sense of relationships and behavioral responses means: to make a bad situation even worse, to say or do something to make someone angry or to stir up or create strong feelings of anger love or hate, to exasperate or aggravate an already explosive situation, to cause or incite strong negative emotions. For example: "The Coronavirus outbreak has fanned the flames of the US and China relations." "The political leader is fanning the flames of racial tension and unrest." "The pandemic has fanned the flames of disparities among communities."

SHADOWS OF THE PAST

In this chapter, we want to deal with fanning the flames of a negative traumatic, toxic, and even abusive relationship. Let the fire go out! Let the past go and move forward! There are certain signs of a toxic relationship. Some of these are: lack of trust, frequent lying, controlling behaviors, all take and no give, hostile communication, feeling drained all the time, and making excuses for their behavior. It's not always easy to tell if you're in a toxic relationship. The problem is that many unhealthy relationships are rooted in our culture. We consider many things normal because it's what we've seen and experienced most of our lives. Abuse to one person might be considered love to another person. Toxic relationships are all about how much stress it puts on you and how much work goes into maintaining the relationship. Obviously, there is a certain amount of work that goes into marriage or any relationship. If you're working all the time to keep the relationship going, then where is the fun? All work and no play (fun) makes for a very unfulfilling relationship. Sometimes it makes for a life of misery.

Accept the fact you are in a difficult stressful, situation and be honest with yourself. Acceptance is the first step. Accept that the relationship is super hard, and you are exhausted from trying to make it work. You're putting in more than you are getting out of the relationship. Acceptance is not always easy. It takes courage to let go of someone you love, but yet the relationship is toxic. You can't avoid the inevitable by continuing a relationship that you know is going nowhere. Accept the fact that letting go is going to be difficult. Come to grips with these facts:

- You deserve better
- Accept that it will hurt
- Happiness is within your control
- Stop waiting on your partner to change
- Accept that sometimes good things can be toxic.

Stop fanning the flames. Let the fire go out. Sometimes love isn't enough to keep you together. Toxic relationships are shadows of the past. You can move from the abuse. It's like putting work and money in an old car that continues to break down. No matter how much money you put in that car it keeps stopping. Now you have to decide whether to continue fixing the car or junking the car for a new more reliable car. When you realize the car is draining all your funds, you start counting up the cost to see if it's really worth it. You have to believe there is better for you. A toxic relationship is not your last hope for love. The time you spend on the wrong person prevents you from meeting the right person.

One of the biggest mistakes is staying in a relationship where you are being mistreated hoping the person will change. After a certain period of time, it becomes evident they will not change, no matter how many times they say they are going to change. You cannot force them. Change has to come from within.

Stop fanning the flames! Accept the fact that your judgment is cloudy when it comes to someone you love. We all want to believe the best when it comes to someone we love. Not all relationships are toxic. Some relationships are just not meant to be. Not all relationships are abusive, yet they are not meant to be. Fanning the flames on the relationship that is not meant to be will only prolong you from doing what you need to do. Somethings don't work out because they are not meant to work out.

Stop fanning the flames because you are afraid of being alone. There will be an adjustment to being single again. That will eventually pass and you will experience the freedom and peace of being in control of your life again. God will give you the strength you need to move forward. You are never alone. Singleness does not mean loneliness. **Isaiah 41:10** says,

> "Fear not, for I am with you, be not dismayed, for I am your God. I will strengthen you , I will help you, I will uphold you with my righteous right hand."

God's word assures us that we are never alone, so don't be afraid to let go.

> **Isaiah 54:10** says, "For the mountains may depart and the hills be removed, but my steadfast love shall not depart from you and my covenant of peace shall not be removed, says the Lord, who has compassion on you."

God has made a covenant of peace with you that shall not be removed. You need to accept his peace today and make steps toward deliverance. **John 14:27** says,

> "Peace I leave with you, my peace I give to you. Not as the world gives do I give to you. Let not your hearts be troubled, neither let them be afraid."

The best is yet to come for you. God has made so many

promises to you in his word. Read them, meditate on them, and you will find peace. The word of God gives us the faith and strength we need to get through any situation or circumstance.

The Bible actually gives us an example of what a healthy relationship should look like.
- Love is patient
- Love is kind
- It does not envy
- It does not boast
- It is not proud
- It does not dishonor others
- It is not self-seeking
- It is not easily angered
- It keeps no record of wrongs
- Love does not delight in evil but rejoices with the truth
- It always protects
- Always trusts
- Always hopes
- Always perseveres (1 Corinthians 13:4-7)

This is the absolute picture of a healthy relationship. If we take the opposite of 1Corinthians 13:4-7, this is what we see:
- Lacks patience
- Is verbally and or physically abusive
- Acts jealous over every little thing
- Boasts excessively
- Is excessively prideful

- Dishonors others
- Is self-seeking
- Reminds others of past mistakes
- Delights in your pain or suffering
- Neglects or refuses to protect or defend you
- Refuses to trust
- Lacks hope
- Gives up easily

Wow! What a contrast. Does this sound like the relationship you're in? Stop fanning the flames! God intentionally revealed the struggles of many of his chosen people in the Bible. It was not to make them look horrible in our eyes but to show us they were human just like us. They were subjected to sin and mistakes and shame just like us. They had serious character flaws just like us. Many of them failed miserably just like us. They blew it just like us and some of them were involved in ungodly, unholy toxic relationships just like us. The good news is after they received the chastisement of the Lord, they repented of their disobedience and changed. Let's take a look at one of these biblical stories, David and Bathsheba.

THE TOXIC COVER UP

"In the spring, at the time when kings go off to war, David sent Joab out with the king's men and the whole Israelite army. They destroyed the Amorites and besieged Rabbah. But David remained in Jerusalem.

"One evening David got up from his bed and walked around on the roof of the palace. From the roof he saw

> *a woman bathing. The woman was very beautiful. And David sent someone to find out about her. The man said, she is Bathsheba, the daughter of Eliam and the wife of Uriah the Hittite. "Then David sent messengers to her. She came to him, and he slept with her. Now she was purifying herself from her monthly uncleanness. Then she went back home. The woman conceived and sent word to David saying, I am pregnant. So David sent this word to Joab. Send me Uriah the Hittite. And Joab sent him to David... So Uriah left the palace, and a gift from the king was sent after him. But Uriah slept at the entrance to the palace with all his master's servants and did not go down to his house. David was told, Uriah did not go home. So he asked Uriah, haven't you just come home from a military campaign? Why didn't you go home?*

> *"Uriah said to David, the ark and Israel and Judah are staying in tents, and my commander Joab and my Lord's men are camped in the open country. How could I go to my house to eat and drink and make love to my wife? As surely as you live, I will not do such a thing!"* **(2 Samuel 11:1-13 NIV)**

The story of David and Bathsheba has "toxic" written all over it. The relationship was so toxic that it led to a major cover-up of the pregnancy and affair, to a major set up of the death of Uriah. There was nothing good about this relationship. David fanned the flames until the fire got too hot. It spread and got out of control. Instead of letting the fire go out, he proceeded in putting more "wood" (the setup of

Uriah and his death) on the fire.

Bathsheba was the daughter of Eliam and was probably of noble birth. She was also beautiful. She was married to Uriah, one of King David's generals. While she was bathing, David saw her and was overcome with lust. The fire had started! After learning she was married, he proceeded to summon her to come to his chambers where they conceived a child. He fans the fire until it set ablaze so to speak. Instead of going out to battle with his men, king David stays at home relaxing and taking another man wife. We're not told in the chapter that Bathsheba made any seductive advances on the King. However, Dave was the king and no woman in his kingdom could resist his power and authority. David was burning with lust. Today's women's movement (MeToo) would say that Bathsheba was a victim of rape. King David abused his power to propagate a "culture" of lies and rape, much like we've seen play out many times in the news. Men of power and wealth have fostered a culture of rape and sex trafficking in the political and entertainment sector.

As the story continues, David further abuses his power to cover up his adulterous affair by having Bathsheba's husband murdered in cold blood. He also had failed attempts in manipulating Uriah to go home and sleep with his wife. Hence, covering up her pregnancy. David was the king that God chose after dethroning Saul. He was God's man. He would be dealt with by God for his sin. The Bible does not hold back from revealing David's sin and character. He was a ruthless, narcissistic ruler that took what he wanted.

Ultimately, David is held accountable for his sin. The prophet Nathan confronts him directly in a prophetic oracle that depicts the king as morally reprehensible. The toxic cover-up gets exposed by God, who has all wisdom, knowledge, and power. He gave the prophet Nathan to speak to David by referencing a story.

> "Now a traveler came to the rich man, but the rich man refrained from taking one of his own sheep or cattle to prepare a meal for the traveler who had come to him. Instead, he took the ewe lamb that belonged to the poor man and prepared it for the one who had come to him. David burned with anger against the man and said to Nathan, As surely as the Lord lives the man who did this must die! He must pay for that lamb four times over, because he did such a thing and had no pity.

> "Then Nathan said to David, You are the man! This is what the Lord said, the God of Israel says, I anointed you king over Israel and I delivered you from the hand of Saul. I gave your master's house to you and your master's wives into your arms. I gave you all Israel and Judah. And if all this had been to little I would have given you even more. Why did you despise the word of the Lord by doing what is evil in his eyes? You struck down Uriah the Hittite with the sword and took his wife to be your own. You killed him with the sword of the Amorites. Now, therefore, the sword will never depart from your house because you despised me and took the wife of Uriah the Hittite to be your own...Then David said to Nathan, I have sinned against the Lord. Nathan replied, the Lord has taken away you're sin. You are not

> going to die. But because by doing this you have shown utter contempt for the Lord, the son born to you will die.
>
> After Nathan had gone home, the Lord struck the child that Uriah's wife had born to David, and he became ill. David pleaded with God for the child. He fasted and spent nights lying in sack cloth on the ground. On the seventh day the child died. Then David comforted his wife Bathsheba and he went to her and made love to her. She gave birth to a son and they named him Solomon." (**2 Samuel Chapter 12 NIV)**

When you fan the flames of a toxic relationship, you suffer the consequences. Do not hesitate to do what you know you have to do. Procrastinating will only make things worse. When you don't cut the strings and break the soul tie, things will proceed to get worse. There is a cause-and-effect for everything that happens in life. David's story is told in great lengths for a reason. You can literally visualize it as it's told in the scriptures in **2 Samuel chapters 11 and 12.** God took David's behavior personal, as a direct sin against Him. He said, "Because you despised me." Can our actions despise the Lord? Absolutely! Can we show contempt for God? Absolutely! David felt the sting of his sin and this toxic relationship. He later wrote the 51st Psalm as a poetic lament for the disgrace he brought upon God and all the people of Israel. The damage was done, but yet God turned this whole tragedy around for good. Because David loved God, and he was sorry for what he had done, he repented.

God can turn it around for you. Don't continue fanning the

flames. Let the fire go out. God's got better things in store for you. It's not too late. When there is a fire, we are instructed to STOP, DROP, and ROLL. STOP fanning the fire, DROP the relationship, and ROLL on.

SHADOWS OF THE PAST

10 YOU'RE GOING TO MAKE IT AFTER ALL

We all know that emotional healing and deliverance can be an uphill battle. That's right, it's a battle, and it's a struggle. It is not for the faint at heart. Be prepared to fight and scratch your way out from under those dark shadows of the past. Believe it or not, you have what it takes to do it. If God be for you, all the dark shadows in the past cannot be against you. **Philippians 4:13 (NLT)** says, *"I can do everything through Christ who gives me strength."* Notice the apostle said "I can." That's an affirmative. He didn't say "I hope I can ," or "Maybe I can." He's positive that he can. Because you have the God, who gives you strength, you can overcome every obstacle and every shadow. You can, and you will be healed, because you are more than a conqueror.

> *"What then, shall we say in response to these things? If God is for us, who can be against us? He who did not spare his own son, but gave him up for us all- how will he not also, along with him, graciously give us all things?" Who will bring any charge against those whom God has chosen? It is God who justifies. Who then is the one who condemns? No one. "Christ Jesus who died - More than that, who was raised to life is at the right hand of God, and is also*

> *interceding for us. Who shall separate us from the love of Christ? Shall trouble or hardship or persecution or famine or nakedness or danger or sword?"*
>
> *"As it is written: For your sake we face death all day long; we are considered as sheep to be slaughtered. No, yet in all these things we are more than conquerors through him who loved us. For I am convinced that neither death nor life, neither angels nor demons, neither the present nor the future, nor any powers, neither heights nor death; nor anything else in all creation will be able to separate us from the love of God that is in Christ Jesus our Lord."* **(Romans 8:35 -39)**

We see Paul asking this question, *"Who can separate us from the love of Christ?"* Take notice to the answer he provides to this question. Instead of simply saying, "No such powerless things can separate us from the love of God, instead he says, "Yet in all these things," meaning that while we are in the midst of our distress, while we are encircled by shadows of the past, while we feel hopeless; in the midst of all this, he says we are more than conquerors!

You are more than a conqueror, because God is with you. He gives you strength, but it doesn't mean you don't have to do anything. God expects you to fight the good fight of faith. All throughout the Bible we see God giving his chosen people Israel, the victory time and time again. Honestly speaking, Israel was no match for their enemies. They were not skilled in war like their enemies. They didn't have all the weapons of war like their enemies. They were outmatched when it came to that perspective. However, Israel had a "secret weapon"

GOD. He was their "ace in the hole." Many times God told them not to be afraid. He would fight their battles for them. **Exodus 14:14** says, *"The Lord shall fight for you, and you shall hold your peace."* Also in **Jeremiah 1:19** it says, *"They will fight against you, but they shall not prevail against you. For I am with you. Says the Lord, to deliver you."*

Just like God is with Israel, so is he with you. God does not wait for you to come out of the battle or the test to affirm that you are more than a conqueror. He calls you "more than a conqueror" while you are in the midst of the fight. The test does not define you; God does. The truth is we can face our shadows of the past because we don't stand on our own authority but on God. You're going to make it after all!

None of us are exempt from suffering. There is no perfect life here on earth. Jesus Christ suffered and bore his own cross and we will also suffer. There is an old song written by Thomas Shepherd, published in 1693. The lyrics say: "Must Jesus bear the cross alone, and all the world go free? No, there's a cross for everyone, and there is a cross for me." **Philippians 1:29 NIV** says, *"For it has been granted to you on behalf of Christ not only to believe in him, but also to suffer for him."* The apostle Paul was one of the greatest apostles of all times. He wrote many of the epistles in the New Testament, yet his life was no walk in the park."

PAUL SEES THE LIGHT

Let's look at the life of the man that gave us so many encouraging books of the Bible to read. The birth name of

Apostle Paul was actually Saul. He was born into a Jewish family in the city of Tarsus. His birth in a Roman "free city" grants him Roman citizenship, a privilege he will exercise later in life. The early religious training Paul receives came from the best rabbinical school in Jerusalem. It was led by the well-known and respected Pharisee, Gamaliel.

Paul was 30 years old when he was an official witness at the stoning of Stephen. His dedication to stopping the early spread of Christianity knew no bounds. He was totally dedicated to stopping the spread of the gospel. After seeing Stephen's life taken, he led the first great wave of persecution against the early church. Paul was like a madman. His dedication to eradicating those believing in the teachings of Jesus lead him to take bold actions, such as going from house to house in order to find believers **(Acts 8:1,3)**.

After his efforts to stop the spread of early Christian believers in Jerusalem, Paul set his sights on achieving this audacious goal of removing any Christian influence in the synagogues of Damascus. He received written permission from the temple High Priest to rid the city's synagogues of any who believed. His intention was to arrest those who believe that Jesus was the Messiah and take them back to Jerusalem for punishment.

It's during his trip to Damascus that the pivotal life-changing event happened. A light from heaven shone on Saul. He heard the voice of Jesus saying, *"Saul, Saul, why do you persecute me?"* **(Acts 9:4)** It was there that the Lord strikes him blind and he had to be led back to the city. These events led to his total repentance and conversion, receiving the gift of the Holy Spirit. God later healed him of his blindness.

After his conversion Paul uses the same zeal he had for persecuting Christians to spreading the good news of Jesus Christ. His amazing ministry lasted 35 years until his death at the age of 66. His accomplishments are astonishing. During his ministry he resurrects at least one person from the dead and is resurrected himself after being stoned to death. Paul carries out at least five evangelistic journeys, visited more than 50 cities in his travels and preaches the gospel to emperor Caesar and his entire household. He also writes no less than 14 books (epistles) of the Bible the most of any author, trains other evangelists like John Mark and Timothy and endures a total of more than five years in prison. The apostle Paul, whose life was cut short by the Romans in 68 A.D. is easily the most influential Christian in the New Testament short of Jesus himself.

This man was as wretched as they came. He had a horrible past. How do you even begin to forget the past? Where do you even start? Paul was a terror, but God had plans for his life. There is nothing too hard for the Lord. If Paul could let go of his deep dark shadows of the past, certainly you can. He found a way to put his shameful past behind him, concentrating on the prize that was set before him.

YOU CAN MAKE IT ON BROKEN PIECES

It is important to note God's providence in all these events concerning Paul. Jesus appears to Paul in Jerusalem.

The following night the Lord stood near Paul and said, *"Take courage. As you have testified about me in Jerusalem, so you must also testify in Rome."* **(Acts 23:11)**

The Roman centurion Julius, was responsible for delivering this prisoner (Paul) and was required to guard him with his life. In fact, Julius treated Paul kindly. For the first time since Paul's earlier arrival in Jerusalem **(Acts 21:17, 18)** Luke, the writer of the book of acts **(Acts 1:1)** begins to include himself once again as a companion of Paul when he recorded, *"We boarded a ship from . . ."* **(Acts 27:2)**. In addition to Luke, Aristarchus joins Paul on the ship as well. The Mediterranean Sea was rough in the winter and the ship Paul and the others first boarded left late in the safe season. In Myra they were transferred to another ship. Stormy weather meant that the ship was not able to take a direct route, so the captain sailed on the east and south sides of Crete and took shelter in a southern port.

The ship never made it to its destination. Storms pushed it well off course and into the Mediterranean. The situation became so desperate that cargo and the ships' tackle were thrown overboard to stay afloat. The storms made the usual navigation by stars impossible, so the ship finally made it to the island of Malta. An angel appeared to Paul and gave him a word from God saying all lives would be spared. The ship later hit a sandbar and began to break up, but all 276 passengers and crew on board made it safely to shore by swimming on floating pieces of board from the wreckage of the ship. They made it on broken pieces. This is interesting.

God told Paul he would go to Rome and be a witness there for Christ, but he didn't tell Paul how he would arrive there. Many times, God makes us a promise but he doesn't tell us how it will come to pass. He chooses to leave out all the details. This is indeed a "faith" walk. *We walk by faith not by sight."* **(2 Corinthians 5:7)**

Paul and the crew made it on broken pieces, but they made it. The ship was a wreck, but there was enough wood for them to drift on. It may seem like your life consists of just broken pieces. You have broken dreams and broken promises people made you. You may even have a broken heart, but you're going to make it. God has made you promises that he's going to fulfill. He cannot lie and he cannot die! You will be healed of the past. You're going to make it after all!

SHADOWS OF THE PAST

CONCLUSION

God is the only one that wants your "junk." He's the only one that can take a bad situation and turn it around for your good. He can take the worst sinner and turn him into a saint. He can take tragedy and turn it into praise. He can take your ashes and give you beauty for them. He takes your garment of heaviness and gives you a garment of praise. He takes our bad, shameful dark past and gives us a glorious future in return. He wants what no one else want. Nothing is ever lost or wasted with God. **Romans 8:28 NIV** says, *"And we know that in all things, God works for the good of those who love him, who have been called according to his purpose."*

The apostle Paul wrote the book of Romans. He begins chapter 8 by discussing the difference between living by the Spirit and living by the flesh. He states that living by the Spirit makes us sons and daughters of God.

> *"The Spirit himself testifies with our spirit that we are God's children. Now if we are children then we are heirs - heirs of God and co-heirs with Christ. If indeed we share in his sufferings, in order that we may also share in his glory. "* **(Romans 8:16,17 NIV)**

Paul compares the sufferings that we face in this life with *"the glory that will be revealed in us."* **(Romans 8:18)**

SHADOWS OF THE PAST

The promise of **Romans 8:28**, that God works for our good in all things, is reassuring. This means that no matter what the circumstances were of your past, God will work all things for your good, if you love him and you are called according to his purpose. We can trust that God will work out all things for our good. He takes the bad and the good and work them together because he sees the big picture.

We are part of God's plan. The Apostle says we have been called according to his purpose. He knows the future, and his desires for us will be accomplished. The providence of God is at work in your life. Things might not have worked out the way you desired, but God is in control. We often have different plans for our lives. That's why you hear people say, "I never thought this would happen to me," or "This was the last thing I wanted to happen." The Bible tells us in **Isaiah 55:8-9 (NIV),** *"For my thoughts are not your thoughts, neither are your ways my ways, declares the Lord. As the heavens are higher than the earth, so are my ways higher than your ways and my thoughts than your thoughts."* We are called according to His plan, not ours. God further declares in his word: "I make known the end from the beginning, from ancient times, what is still to come. I say, *"My purpose will stand, and I will do all that I please."* **(Isaiah 46:10)**

This is so powerful. God has made known our end from the very beginning. He's already decided how your life will play out, and what has not happened is already determined. He concludes by saying, *"My purpose (plan) will stand, and I will do all that I please."* Even when things seem chaotic and

CONCLUSION

out of control, God is still in charge. He's in charge even when you are struggling, even when your life is upside down, and even when you're at your lowest. There are times when we are afraid and anxious about our future. It is at that moment we need to cast all our cares on him. Honestly, we don't know where we're going from day to day. We make plans but life does not always go along with our plans. We can't see into tomorrow, but God can. He's already into tomorrow, and the next day, and the next day, in the future. He's omnipresent. He's everywhere, past, present, and future - all at once. This is why we must trust him. He always has our best interest in mind. **Jeremiah 29:11, 12** says,

> "For I know the plans I have for you declares the Lord. Plans to prosper you and not to harm you, plans to give you hope and a future. Then you will call upon me and come and pray to me, and I will listen to you. You will seek me and find me when you seek me with all your heart."

There is a historical and literary context that we need to understand in the above passage of scripture. For historical context, Jeremiah spoke these words to Jews who had been living under domination of the Egyptian and then Babylonian empires before eventually being carried into exile from Jerusalem to Babylon. You can only imagine what it would be like to live under the domination of your enemies and then be forced by those enemies to leave your homeland and settle in a foreign land.

For literary context, we discover from the previous

chapter that Jeremiah had just pronounced judgment upon the false prophet Hananiah. Hananiah told the people that God would break the yoke of Babylon, freeing the people to return home, within two years. While this message sounded appealing to the people, it was a lie and it resulted in God removing Hananiah from the face of the earth. **(Jeremiah 28:15-17)**

Instead, Jeremiah tells the people they would live in Babylon for at least 70 years. They were instructed to settle down, build houses, marry and even pray for the peace and prosperity of the city in which they now found themselves. **(Jeremiah 28:4 -10)**

In context, we discover that the words of **Jeremiah 29:11** were spoken to people in the midst of hardship and suffering, people who were likely desiring an immediate rescue like the one Hananiah lied about. But God does not always promise an immediate escape from the difficult situation. Rather, he promises he has a plan to prosper them in the midst of their current situation. We can all take comfort in **Jeremiah 29:11,** knowing that a promise is a promise, and God always keeps his promises. God will work through whatever it is that you are working through. He has promised you hope and a future. The Lord speaks to you now and say:

> *"So do not fear, for I am with you, do not be dismayed, for I am your God. I will strengthen you and help you. I will uphold you with my righteous right hand."* **(Isaiah 41:10)**

CONCLUSION

SHALOM!

SHADOWS OF THE PAST

ABOUT THE AUTHORS

Drs. Curt and Linda Stennis are pastors, teachers, authors, conference speakers, and business consultants. They preach a clear and concise life changing message. Their anointed teaching and preaching include illustrations that causes manifestations and importations. They challenge individuals to move beyond complacency and pursue excellence in every area of life.

Dr. Curt and Dr. Linda are the founding Pastors of **Salvation and Deliverance Ministries International** of Chicago Illinois and Oakbrook Terrace (1983); Apostles and Overseers of **In Covenant Ministries Fellowship** (2007), a global ministry of clergy, civic and business leaders; and founders of **Covenant Keepers Bible Institute**. Together, Drs. Curt and Linda are a dynamic team - whether ministering in national and international conferences, revivals, seminars or business expos. They have conducted conferences and seminars in East Africa (Kenya and Uganda) and West Africa (Ghana). Other travels include but are not limited to Venezuela, Mexico, El Salvador, Puerto Rico and other Central and South American countries. They oversee over 100 churches in these nations.

Drs. Curt and Linda Stennis are authors and publishers of numerous books including bestsellers **"But God, You Promised,"** **"Help Lord, The Devil Wants Me Broke"** and **"Momentum – The Cutting Edge for Winning."** They are also editors of **"The Set Times Magazine."** Their multifaceted ministries, as well as business ventures and civic involvement, have produced television interviews, newspaper articles and many awards.

You may contact Drs. Curt and Linda for future ministry or business consultation.

Salvation and Deliverance Ministries International
In Covenant Ministries Fellowship
Alpha & Omega Innovative Publishing
2005 South Meyers Rd, Unit 235
Oak Brook Terrace, Illinois 60181
630-326-7451

Email: sdmichicago7@gmail.com
Facebook: @ SDMIChurch

All of their books are available at Amazon.com
https://www.amazon.com/Curt-and-Linda-Stennis

BEST SELLER BY DRS. CURT AND LINDA STENNIS!

"Sometimes we forget how faithful our God is. Drs. Curtis and Linda Stennis remind us in this book that the One who has made the promises in the Bible keeps His Word."

Dr. Richard Roberts, President
Oral Roberts Ministries
Tulsa, Oklahoma

"BUT GOD...YOU PROMISED! is a "Promise-full," Powerful Book. I consider this book a must-read."

Apostle Dr. Jo Ann Long
New Covenant Life Church
Chicago, Illinois

"One can see how God has blessed Drs. Curtis and Linda Stennis with the God kind of faith, thereby enabling them to live the abundant life."

Dr. Mildred C. Harris, President
God First Ministries
Chicago, Illinois

"After reading this book, it will challenge you to remove all the pre-conceived notions in your life and obtain the things that God promised you."

Dr. Kervin J. Smith
Kervin Smith Ministries
Eden Prairie, Minnesota

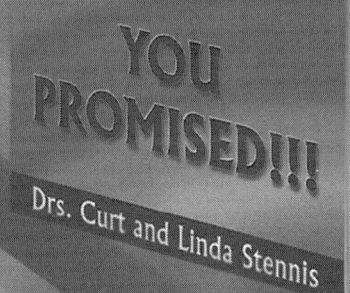

Order your copy from
aoinnovativepublishing.com

The devil wages a war to keep money and resources out of the hands of God's people!

HELP LORD!
the devil wants me

BROKE!
CURT AND LINDA STENNIS

A TIMELY PUBLICATION
BY DRS. CURT AND LINDA STENNIS

It is God's divine will that his people prosper in every area of their lives!

In this new book, you will discover vital keys to prosperity and good success. You will discover Kingdom Principles that will break the cycle of lack and insufficiency. These divine principles will propel you into the arena of abundance and the blessings that overflow!

ORDER YOUR COPY TODAY
GO TO WWW.AOINNOVATIVEPUBLISHING.COM
ALPHA & OMEGA INNOVATIVE PUBLISHING - CHICAGO, ILLINOIS

Introducing

Spiritually, and prophetically speaking, acceleration has come to the Body of Christ. Momentum is in our favor!
Receive the cutting edge power for winning!

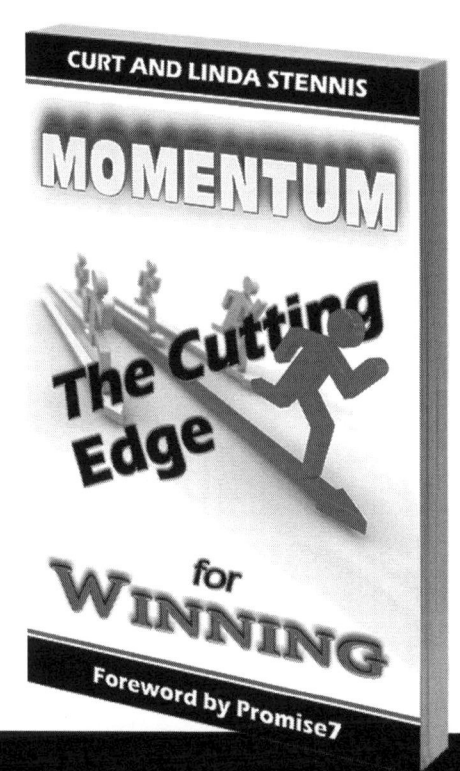

CURT AND LINDA STENNIS

MOMENTUM
The Cutting Edge for WINNING
Foreword by Promise7

Drs. Curt and Linda Stennis clearly display to their readers how to develop an attainable plan that will propel you from mediocre to the cutting edge, out of the box, arena of winning. They also offer instructions on how to avoid certain hinders that block your MOMENTUM. Their dynamic revelation of this indescribable, powerful driving force called MOMENTUM is absolutely God influenced and God inspired.

A Ω
ALPHA & OMEGA
INNOVATIVE PUBLISHING

For more information and to order, go to www.promise7.org or www.aoinnovativepublishing.com

Alpha and Omega Innovative Publishing
presents

The New Book Release by Dr. Curt Stennis

CURT STENNIS

Resounding **GRACE**

An In Depth Study Of the Grace of God

foreword by **LINDA STENNIS**

For more information and to order your copy go to www.aoinnovativepublishing.com or facebook.com/aoinnovativepublishers
312-671-2631

ALPHA & OMEGA INNOVATIVE PUBLISHING

"Illuminating your Vision from Beginning to End"

Dr. Linda Stennis

MAY I BORROW A CUP OF SUGAR?
PROPHETIC INSIGHT ON KINGDOM CONNECTIONS
LINDA STENNIS

"This book is unique, captivating, and thorough in describing that many Kingdom Connections are as close and simple as taking a step to "Borrow a Cup of Sugar" from a neighbor. This is a powerful analogy with great scriptural support, awesome revelation, and keen prophetic insight that only a prophetic gift like her could conceive. Expect a new awareness, expect a distinct new position in your life, new strategies in business, new avenues, and yes, new Kingdom Connections."
Dr. Curt Stennis

Alpha and Omega Innovative Publishing
Presents

CULTURE SHOCK
THE ELEMENTS THAT MAKE UP A CULTURE

CURT AND LINDA STENNIS

JUST WHEN I THOUGHT I COULDN'T BE SHOCKED!

#CULTURESHOCK

AVAILABLE NOW ON AMAZON!
www.aoinnovativepublishing.com
or facebook.com/aoinnovativepublishers
312-671-2631

ALPHA & OMEGA
INNOVATIVE PUBLISHING

"Illuminating your Vision from Beginning to End"

ALPHA AND OMEGA INNOVATIVE PUBLISHING
PRESENTS

WHAT DO I DO WHEN SHIFT HAPPENS?

DRS. CURT AND LINDA STENNIS

LINDA STENNIS

WHAT DO I DO WHEN SHIFT HAPPENS?

CURT STENNIS

We are so excited about this book: "What Do I Do When Shift Happens?" This powerful revelation will hopefully clarify some misconcepts of the trendy words, "There is a shift taking place in your life...", "God is shifting you...", God is shifting the atmosphere..." What exactly does that mean? What am I supposed to do after getting a prophetic word like that? When God has predestined you for greater, you need to "shift." Another word for shift is "change." You have the ability to change the direction your life is going, and you have the ability to change what you don't like. Shifting can be immediate or it can be a process. We make shifts in life from bad to better, from poor to rich, from small to great and from better to best. Several shifts are evident in your life. God can shift you, the economy can shift you and you can shift yourself. God's shift is setting you up for prosperity and good success. "For all the promises of God find their yes in Him."

Drs. Curt and Linda Stennis are Apostles, Pastors, international conference speakers, authors, publishers, entrepreneurs, and business consultants. They are founders of Salvation and Deliverance Ministries International and in Covenant Ministries Fellowship in Chicago.

For over 3 decades their apostolic ministry has spanned the globe ministering to 5 fold ministry gifts, civic and business leaders. Their teaching and preaching is unique, life-changing, revelatory and relevant to everyday issues bringing help and hope to individuals.

ISBN 978-0-9890817-1-7

AVAILABLE NOW ON AMAZON!
www.aoinnovativepublishing.com
facebook.com/aoinnovativepublishers
312-671-2631

ALPHA & OMEGA
INNOVATIVE PUBLISHING

"Illuminating your Vision from Beginning to End"

Declaring The End... From The Beginning

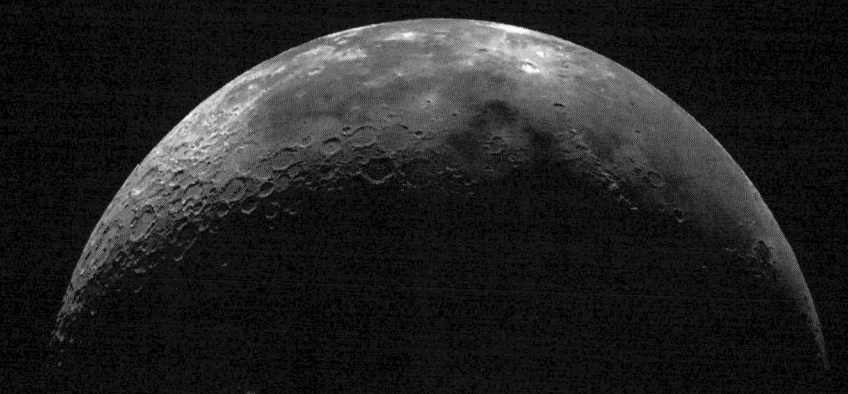

God's Prophetic Plan

LINDA STENNIS

Alpha & Omega Innovative Publishing

Illuminating your Vision From Beginning to End

WWW.AOINNOVATIVEPUBLISHING.COM
WWW.AOINNOVATIVEBOOKSTORE.COM

312-671-2631

THE PERFECT STORM

Jonah's Dilemma

Curt Stennis